S0-AEH-702

Publications International, Ltd.

Favorite Brand Name Recipes at www.fbnr.com

Copyright © 2003 Publications International, Ltd.
All rights reserved. This publication may not be reproduced or quoted in whole or in part by any means whatsoever without written permission from:

Louis Weber, CEO
Publications International, Ltd.
7373 North Cicero Avenue
Lincolnwood, IL 60712

Permission is never granted for commercial purposes.

All recipes and photographs that contain specific brand names are copyrighted by those companies and/or associations, unless otherwise specified. All photographs *except* those on pages 37, 87, 107, 117, 149, 171, 201, 209, 213, 253, 259, 297, 323 and 341 copyright © Publications International, Ltd.

BISQUICK is a registered trademark of General Mills, Inc.

DOLE® is a registered trademark of Dole Food Company, Inc.

™/© M&M's, M and the M&M's Characters are trademarks of Mars, Incorporated.
© Mars, Inc. 2003.

Nestlé, Ortega and Toll House are registered trademarks of Nestlé.

Butter Flavor CRISCO® all-vegetable shortening and Butter Flavor CRISCO® No-Stick Cooking Spray are artificially flavored.

Some of the products listed in this publication may be in limited distribution.

Pictured on the front cover *(clockwise from top left):* Velveeta® Ultimate Macaroni & Cheese *(page 144),* Bittersweet Pecan Brownies with Caramel Sauce *(page 346),* Potato Soup with Green Chilies & Cheese *(page 156)* and Buttermilk Ranch Fried Chicken *(page 25).*

Pictured on the back cover *(clockwise from top left):* Apricot Pork Chop and Dressing *(page 72),* Potatoes au Gratin *(page 178)*, Spiced Cranberry-Apple Sour Cream Cobbler *(page 314)* and S'more Snack Treats *(page 360).*

ISBN: 0-7853-7746-8

Library of Congress Control Number: 2002112008

Manufactured in China.

8 7 6 5 4 3 2 1

Microwave Cooking: Microwave ovens vary in wattage. Use the cooking times as guidelines and check for doneness before adding more time.

Preparation/Cooking Times: Preparation times are based on the approximate amount of time required to assemble the recipe before cooking, baking, chilling or serving. These times include preparation steps such as measuring, chopping and mixing. The fact that some preparations and cooking can be done simultaneously is taken into account. Preparation of optional ingredients and serving suggestions is not included.

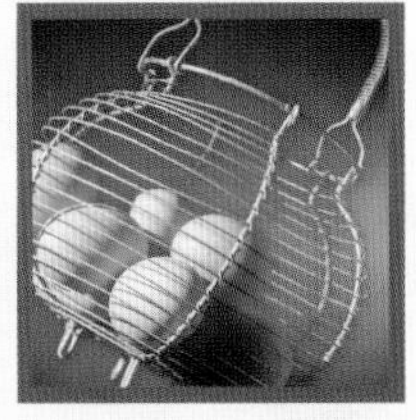

Contents

Roast Chicken with Peppers

1 chicken (3 to 3½ pounds), cut into pieces
3 tablespoons olive oil, divided
1½ tablespoons chopped fresh rosemary *or* 1½ teaspoons dried rosemary, crushed
1 tablespoon fresh lemon juice
1¼ teaspoons salt, divided
¾ teaspoon freshly ground black pepper, divided
3 bell peppers (preferably 1 red, 1 yellow and 1 green)
1 medium onion

1. Heat oven to 375°F. Rinse chicken in cold water; pat dry with paper towel. Place in shallow roasting pan.

2. Combine 2 tablespoons oil, rosemary and lemon juice; brush over chicken. Sprinkle 1 teaspoon salt and ½ teaspoon pepper over chicken. Roast 15 minutes.

3. Cut bell peppers lengthwise into ½-inch thick strips. Slice onion into thin wedges. Toss vegetables with remaining 1 tablespoon oil, ¼ teaspoon salt and ¼ teaspoon pepper. Spoon vegetables around chicken; roast until vegetables are tender and chicken is no longer pink in center, about 40 minutes. Serve chicken with vegetables and pan juices.

Makes 6 servings

Roast Chicken with Peppers

Savory Chicken & Biscuits

2 tablespoons olive or vegetable oil
1 pound boneless skinless chicken breasts or thighs, cut into 1-inch pieces (about 2 cups)
1 medium onion, chopped
1 cup thinly sliced carrots
1 cup thinly sliced celery
1 envelope LIPTON® RECIPE SECRETS® Savory Herb with Garlic Soup Mix*
1 cup milk
1 package (10 ounces) refrigerated flaky buttermilk biscuits

**Also terrific with LIPTON® RECIPE SECRETS® Golden Onion Soup Mix.*

Preheat oven to 400°F.

In 12-inch skillet, heat oil over medium-high heat and cook chicken, stirring occasionally, 5 minutes or until almost done. Stir in onion, carrots and celery; cook, stirring occasionally, 3 minutes. Stir in savory herb with garlic soup mix blended with milk. Bring to the boiling point over medium-high heat, stirring occasionally; cook 1 minute.

Turn into lightly greased 2-quart casserole; arrange biscuits on top of chicken mixture with edges touching. Bake 10 minutes or until biscuits are golden brown.

Makes about 4 servings

Menu Suggestion: Serve with a mixed green salad and LIPTON® Iced Tea.

Savory Chicken & Biscuits

Chicken Gumbo

Prep Time: 15 minutes
Cook Time: 40 minutes

2 tablespoons all-purpose flour
2 teaspoons blackened seasoning mix or Creole seasoning mix
12 ounces boneless skinless chicken thighs, cut into ¾-inch pieces
2 teaspoons olive oil
1 large onion, coarsely chopped
½ cup sliced celery
2 teaspoons minced garlic
1 can (about 14 ounces) reduced-sodium chicken broth
1 can (14½ ounces) no-salt-added stewed tomatoes, undrained
1 large green bell pepper, cut into chunks
1 teaspoon filé powder (optional)
2 cups hot cooked rice
2 tablespoons chopped fresh parsley

1. Combine flour and blackened seasoning mix in large resealable plastic food storage bag. Add chicken; toss to coat. Heat oil in large deep nonstick skillet or saucepan over medium heat. Add chicken to skillet; sprinkle with any remaining flour mixture. Cook and stir 3 minutes. Add onion, celery and garlic; cook and stir 3 minutes.

2. Add chicken broth, tomatoes and bell pepper; bring to a boil. Reduce heat; cover and simmer 20 minutes or until vegetables are tender. Uncover; simmer 5 to 10 minutes or until sauce is slightly reduced. Remove from heat; stir in filé powder, if desired. Ladle into shallow bowls; top with rice and parsley. *Makes 4 (1½-cup) servings*

Note: Filé powder, made from dried sassafras leaves, thickens and flavors gumbos. Look for it in the herb and spice section of your supermarket.

Chicken Gumbo

Country Roasted Chicken Dinner

1 envelope LIPTON® RECIPE SECRETS® Savory Herb with Garlic Soup Mix*
2 tablespoons honey
1 tablespoon water
1 tablespoon I CAN'T BELIEVE IT'S NOT BUTTER!® Spread, melted
1 roasting chicken (5 to 6 pounds)
3 pounds all-purpose and/or sweet potatoes, cut into chunks

**Also terrific with LIPTON® RECIPE SECRETS® Golden Herb with Lemon or Golden Onion Soup Mix.*

Preheat oven to 350°F.

In small bowl, blend savory herb with garlic soup mix, honey, water and I CAN'T BELIEVE IT'S NOT BUTTER!® Spread.

In 18×12-inch roasting pan, arrange chicken, breast side up; brush with soup mixture. Cover loosely with aluminum foil. Roast 30 minutes; drain off drippings. Arrange potatoes around chicken and continue roasting covered, stirring potatoes occasionally, 1 hour or until meat thermometer reaches 175°F and potatoes are tender. *If chicken reaches 175°F before potatoes are tender, remove chicken to serving platter and keep warm. Continue roasting potatoes until tender.*

Makes about 8 servings

Note: For best results, insert meat thermometer into thickest part of thigh between breast and thigh; make sure tip does not touch bone.

Serving Suggestion: Serve with a mixed green salad, warm biscuits and LIPTON® Iced Tea.

Country Roasted Chicken Dinner

Chicken and Homemade Noodle Soup

¾ cup all-purpose flour
2 teaspoons finely chopped fresh thyme *or* ½ teaspoon dried thyme leaves, divided
¼ teaspoon salt
1 egg yolk, beaten
3 tablespoons cold water
1 pound boneless skinless chicken thighs, cut into ½- to ¾-inch pieces
2 cups cold water
5 cups chicken broth
1 medium onion, chopped
1 medium carrot, thinly sliced
¾ cup frozen peas
Chopped fresh parsley for garnish

1. To prepare noodles, stir together flour, 1 teaspoon thyme and salt in small bowl. Add egg yolk and 3 tablespoons water. Stir together until mixed. Shape into small ball. Place dough on lightly floured surface; flatten slightly. Knead 5 minutes or until dough is smooth and elastic, adding more flour to prevent sticking if necessary. Cover with plastic wrap. Let stand 15 minutes.

2. Roll out dough to ⅛-inch thickness or thinner on lightly floured surface with lightly floured rolling pin. If dough is too elastic, let rest a few minutes. Let rolled out dough stand about 30 minutes to dry slightly. Cut into ¼-inch-wide strips. Cut strips 1½ to 2 inches long; set aside.

3. Combine chicken and 2 cups water in medium saucepan. Bring to a boil over high heat. Reduce heat to medium-low; cover and simmer 5 minutes. Drain and rinse chicken; set aside. Combine chicken broth, onion, carrot and remaining 1 teaspoon thyme in 5-quart Dutch oven or large saucepan. Bring to a boil over high heat. Add noodles. Reduce heat to medium-low; simmer, uncovered, 8 minutes or until noodles are tender. Stir in chicken and peas. Bring soup just to a boil. Sprinkle parsley over each serving.

Makes 4 servings

Chicken and Homemade Noodle Soup

Mom's Best Chicken Tetrazzini

8 ounces uncooked vermicelli or thin noodles
2 tablespoons butter
8 ounces fresh mushrooms, sliced
¼ cup chopped green onions
1 can (about 14 ounces) chicken broth
1 cup half-and-half, divided
2 tablespoons dry sherry
¼ cup all-purpose flour
½ teaspoon salt
¼ teaspoon ground nutmeg
⅛ teaspoon white pepper
1 jar (2 ounces) chopped pimiento, drained
½ cup (4 ounces) grated Parmesan cheese, divided
½ cup sour cream
2 cups cubed cooked chicken

1. Preheat oven to 350°F. Cook noodles according to package directions. Drain; set aside.

2. Melt butter in large nonstick skillet over medium-high heat. Add mushrooms and onions; cook and stir until onions are tender. Add chicken broth, ½ cup half-and-half and sherry to onion mixture. Pour remaining ½ cup half-and-half into small jar with tight-fitting lid; add flour, salt, nutmeg and pepper. Shake well. Slowly stir flour mixture into skillet. Bring to a boil; cook 1 minute. Reduce heat; stir in pimiento and ¼ cup Parmesan cheese. Stir in sour cream; blend well. Add chicken and noodles; mix well.

3. Coat 1½-quart casserole with nonstick cooking spray. Pour mixture into prepared casserole. Sprinkle with remaining ¼ cup Parmesan cheese. Bake 30 to 35 minutes until hot.

Makes 6 servings

Chicken Breasts Fricassee

Prep Time: 15 minutes
Cook Time: 20 minutes

4 boneless, skinless chicken breast halves (about 1¼ pounds)
¼ cup all-purpose flour
¼ teaspoon salt
Dash ground black pepper
2 tablespoons BERTOLLI® Olive Oil
1 tablespoon I CAN'T BELIEVE IT'S NOT BUTTER!® Spread
1 clove garlic, finely chopped
1 cup sliced mushrooms
½ cup chopped onion
¼ cup dry white wine
2 cups water
1 package LIPTON® Rice & Sauce—Chicken Flavor
½ cup frozen green peas, thawed

Dip chicken in flour combined with salt and pepper.

In 12-inch skillet, heat oil over medium heat and cook chicken 5 minutes or until chicken is no longer pink in center, turning once. Remove to serving platter; keep warm.

In same skillet, add I CAN'T BELIEVE IT'S NOT BUTTER!® Spread, garlic, mushrooms and onion and cook over medium heat, stirring occasionally, 3 minutes or until mushrooms are tender. Add wine and boil 30 seconds. Add water and bring to a boil. Stir in Rice & Sauce—Chicken Flavor. Reduce heat and simmer, stirring occasionally, 10 minutes or until rice is tender. Stir in peas and heat through. Garnish, if desired, with chopped parsley. Serve with chicken.

Makes about 4 servings

Classic Fried Chicken

¾ cup all-purpose flour
1 teaspoon salt
¼ teaspoon pepper
1 frying chicken (2½ to 3 pounds), cut up
½ cup CRISCO® Oil*

**Use your favorite Crisco Oil product.*

1. Combine flour, salt and pepper in paper or plastic bag. Add a few pieces of chicken at a time. Shake to coat.

2. Heat oil to 365°F in electric skillet or on medium-high heat in large heavy skillet. Fry chicken 30 to 40 minutes without lowering heat until no longer pink in center. Turn once for even browning. Drain on paper towels. *Makes 4 servings*

Note: For thicker crust, increase flour to 1½ cups. Shake damp chicken in seasoned flour. Place on waxed paper. Let stand for 5 to 20 minutes before frying.

Spicy Fried Chicken: Increase pepper to ½ teaspoon. Combine pepper with ½ teaspoon poultry seasoning, ½ teaspoon paprika, ½ teaspoon cayenne pepper and ¼ teaspoon dry mustard. Rub on chicken before step 1. Substitute 2¼ teaspoons garlic salt, ¼ teaspoon salt and ¼ teaspoon celery salt for 1 teaspoon salt. Combine with flour in step 1 and proceed as directed above.

Classic Fried Chicken

Pan-Fried Stuffed Chicken

1/3 cup diced sweet onion
2 tablespoons chopped fresh parsley
2 tablespoons grated Parmesan cheese
1/2 teaspoon salt
1/4 teaspoon pepper
1/4 teaspoon garlic powder
1/4 teaspoon paprika
4 (1-ounce) slices Swiss cheese
4 boneless, skinless chicken breasts halves, pounded to 1/8-inch thickness
1/2 cup seasoned dry bread crumbs
2 tablespoons grated Parmesan cheese
1/3 cup all-purpose flour
2 eggs, lightly beaten
1/2 cup WESSON® Vegetable Oil

In a small bowl, combine *first* 7 ingredients, ending with paprika; mix well and set aside. Place 1 slice of cheese in center of *each* chicken breast. Top with 1/4 onion mixture. Starting with long edge, tightly roll breast, folding in ends to seal. Secure with toothpicks. In a small bowl, combine bread crumbs and 2 tablespoons Parmesan cheese. Dredge *each* breast in flour. Dip *each* breast in egg and then roll in bread crumbs. In a large skillet, heat Wesson® Oil over medium heat. Fry chicken, starting with seam sides down 20 to 30 minutes or until golden brown and juices run clear, rotating 7 to 10 minutes to avoid overbrowning. Drain on paper towels. Cut chicken crosswise into slices.

Makes 4 servings

Tip: Impress everyone even when you're busy. Chicken can be wrapped individually and frozen up to 2 months. Simply defrost and proceed with the recipe.

Pan-Fried Stuffed Chicken

Chicken Pot Pie

2 teaspoons margarine
½ cup plus 2 tablespoons chicken broth, divided
2 cups sliced mushrooms
1 cup diced red bell pepper
½ cup chopped onion
½ cup chopped celery
2 tablespoons all-purpose flour
½ cup half-and-half
2 cups cubed cooked chicken breasts
1 teaspoon minced fresh dill
½ teaspoon salt
¼ teaspoon black pepper
2 refrigerated crescent rolls

1. Heat margarine and 2 tablespoons chicken broth in medium saucepan until margarine is melted. Add mushrooms, bell pepper, onion and celery. Cook 7 to 10 minutes or until vegetables are tender, stirring frequently.

2. Stir in flour; cook 1 minute. Stir in remaining ½ cup chicken broth; cook and stir until liquid thickens. Reduce heat and stir in half-and-half. Add chicken, dill, salt and pepper.

3. Preheat oven to 375°F. Spoon mixture into greased 1-quart casserole. Roll out crescent rolls and place on top of chicken mixture.

4. Bake pot pie 20 minutes or until topping is golden and filling is bubbly.

Makes 4 (1-cup) servings

Note: For 2 cups cubed cooked chicken breast, gently simmer 3 small chicken breast halves in 2 cups reduced-sodium chicken broth about 20 minutes or until meat is no longer pink in center. Cool and cut into cubes. If desired, reserve chicken broth for pot pie.

Chicken Pot Pie

Crispy Baked Chicken

8 ounces (1 cup) French onion dip
Milk
1 cup cornflake crumbs
½ cup wheat germ
6 skinless chicken breast halves or thighs (about 1½ pounds)

1. Preheat oven to 350°F. Spray shallow baking pan with nonstick cooking spray.

2. Place dip in shallow bowl; stir until smooth. Add milk, 1 tablespoon at a time, until pourable consistency is reached.

3. Combine cornflake crumbs and wheat germ on plate.

4. Dip chicken pieces in milk mixture; then roll in cornflake mixture. Place chicken in single layer in prepared pan. Bake 45 to 50 minutes or until juices run clear when pierced with fork and chicken is no longer pink near the bone. *Makes 6 servings*

Skillet Roasted Chicken

1 PERDUE® Fresh Young Chicken (3½ to 4½ pounds)
Salt and ground pepper to taste
½ teaspoon paprika
1 to 2 tablespoons butter or margarine, softened
1 can (10¾ ounces) low-sodium chicken broth
Juice of ½ lemon (about 2 tablespoons)

Preheat oven to 375°F. Remove giblets from chicken and reserve for another use. Split chicken down backbone and press down on breast to flatten. Place chicken, breast-side up, in large ovenproof skillet or baking pan. Season with salt, pepper and paprika, and dot with butter. Roast, uncovered, 30 minutes, or until chicken begins to brown. Pour in chicken broth and lemon juice. Baste chicken and continue to roast 45 to 60 minutes longer, until skin is a rich, deep brown and juices run clear when thigh is pierced, basting occasionally. A meat thermometer inserted in thickest part of thigh should register 180°F. *Makes 4 servings*

Crispy Baked Chicken

Swiss 'n' Chicken Casserole

Prep Time: 20 minutes
Cook Time: 40 minutes

4 cups chopped cooked chicken
2 cups KRAFT® Shredded Swiss Cheese
2 cups croutons
2 cups sliced celery
1 cup MIRACLE WHIP® or MIRACLE WHIP® LIGHT Dressing
½ cup milk
¼ cup chopped onion
Chopped walnuts (optional)

• Heat oven to 350°F.

• Mix all ingredients except walnuts. Spoon into 2-quart casserole. Sprinkle with walnuts, if desired.

• Bake 40 minutes or until thoroughly heated.

Makes 6 servings

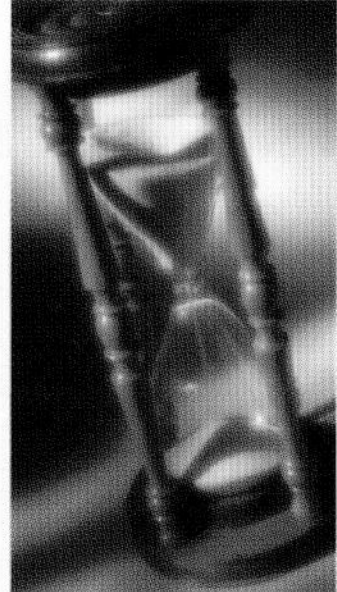

Quick Tip

To speed up preparation, keep packages of 1 or 2 cups of chopped cooked chicken in the freezer. Defrost chicken in microwave oven when needed. Purchase already shredded cheese and chopped walnuts.

Buttermilk Ranch Fried Chicken

2½ to 3 pounds frying chicken pieces
WESSON® Vegetable Oil
2¼ cups all-purpose flour
1¼ tablespoons dried dill weed
1½ teaspoons salt
¾ teaspoon pepper
2½ cups buttermilk

Rinse chicken and pat dry; set aside. Fill a large deep-fry pot or electric skillet to no more than half its depth with Wesson® Oil. Heat oil to 325°F to 350°F. In a medium bowl, combine flour, dill, salt and pepper. Fill another bowl with buttermilk. Place chicken, one piece at a time, in buttermilk; shake off excess liquid. Coat lightly in flour mixture; shake off excess flour. Dip once again in buttermilk and flour mixture. Fry chicken, a few pieces at a time, skin side down, for 10 to 14 minutes. Turn chicken and fry 12 to 15 minutes longer or until juices run clear; drain on paper towels. Let stand 7 minutes before serving. *Makes 4 to 6 servings*

Tip: To reduce frying time by 7 to 9 minutes per side, simply cook unbreaded chicken in boiling water for 15 minutes; remove and cool completely before proceeding with recipe.

Quick Chicken Pot Pie

1 pound boneless skinless chicken thighs, cut into 1-inch cubes
1 can (about 14 ounces) chicken broth
3 tablespoons all-purpose flour
2 tablespoons butter, softened
1 package (10 ounces) frozen mixed vegetables, thawed
1 can (about 4 ounces) button mushrooms, drained
¼ teaspoon dried basil leaves
¼ teaspoon dried oregano leaves
¼ teaspoon dried thyme leaves
1 cup biscuit baking mix
6 tablespoons milk

1. Preheat oven to 450°F. Place chicken and broth in large skillet; cover and bring to a boil over high heat. Reduce heat to medium; simmer, uncovered, 5 minutes or until chicken is tender.

2. While chicken is cooking, mix flour and butter; set aside. Combine mixed vegetables, mushrooms, basil, oregano and thyme in greased 2-quart casserole.

3. Add flour mixture to chicken and broth in skillet; stir with wire whisk until smooth. Cook and stir until thickened. Add to vegetable mixture; mix well.

4. Blend biscuit mix and milk in medium bowl until smooth. Drop 4 scoops of batter onto chicken mixture.

5. Bake 18 to 20 minutes or until biscuits are browned and casserole is hot and bubbly.

Makes 4 servings

Tip: This dish can be prepared through step 3, covered and refrigerated up to 24 hours, if desired. Proceed with step 4; bake as directed for 20 to 25 minutes.

Quick Chicken Pot Pie

Chicken Casserole Olé

12 boneless, skinless chicken tenders
2 cups water
1 can (15 ounces) mild chili beans, undrained
1 cup salsa
½ cup chopped green bell pepper
2 cups UNCLE BEN'S® Instant Rice
2 cups (8 ounces) shredded Mexican cheese blend, divided
2 cups bite-size tortilla chips

1. Spray large skillet with nonstick cooking spray. Add chicken; cook over medium-high heat 12 to 15 minutes or until lightly browned on both sides and chicken is no longer pink in center.

2. Add water, beans with liquid, salsa and bell pepper. Bring to a boil; add rice and 1 cup cheese. Cover; remove from heat and let stand 5 minutes or until liquid is absorbed. Top with tortilla chips and remaining 1 cup cheese; let stand, covered, 3 to 5 minutes or until cheese is melted.

Makes 6 servings

Cheesy Casserole

1½ cups skim milk
1 can (10¾ ounces) condensed cream of chicken soup
1 package (16 ounces) frozen mixed vegetables (thaw and drain)
2 cups finely diced, cooked chicken, turkey or ham
1 cup uncooked instant rice
¾ cup (3 ounces) shredded cheddar cheese
¼ cup grated fresh Parmesan cheese
½ teaspoon LAWRY'S® Garlic Powder with Parsley
½ teaspoon LAWRY'S® Seasoned Pepper
1 tablespoon crushed potato chips or crumbled corn flakes

Lightly grease 9-inch square baking dish. Add milk and soup to dish; mix well with wire whisk. Stir in vegetables, chicken, rice, ½ cup cheddar cheese, 2 tablespoons Parmesan cheese, Garlic Powder with Parsley, and Seasoned Pepper; cover. Bake in 350°F oven 30 minutes. Combine remaining ¼ cup cheddar cheese, 2 tablespoons Parmesan cheese and potato chips; sprinkle over top of casserole. Bake, uncovered, 15 minutes longer.

Makes 4 servings

Chicken Casserole Olé

Chicken and Black Bean Enchiladas

Prep Time: 45 minutes
Cook Time: 25 minutes

2 jars (16 ounces each) mild picante sauce
¼ cup chopped fresh cilantro
2 tablespoons chili powder
1 teaspoon ground cumin
2 cups (10 ounces) chopped cooked chicken
1 can (15 ounces) black beans, drained and rinsed
1⅓ cups *French's®* French Fried Onions, divided
1 package (about 10 ounces) flour tortillas (7 inches)
1 cup (4 ounces) shredded Monterey Jack cheese with jalapeño peppers

Preheat oven to 350°F. Grease 15×10-inch jelly-roll baking pan. Combine picante sauce, cilantro, chili powder and cumin in large saucepan. Bring to a boil. Reduce heat to low; simmer 5 minutes.

Combine 1½ cups sauce mixture, chicken, beans and ⅔ *cup* French Fried Onions in medium bowl. Spoon a scant ½ cup filling over bottom third of each tortilla. Roll up tortillas enclosing filling and arrange, seam side down, in a single layer in bottom of prepared baking pan. Spoon remaining sauce evenly over tortillas.

Bake, uncovered, 20 minutes or until heated through. Sprinkle with remaining ⅔ *cup* onions and cheese. Bake 5 minutes or until cheese is melted and onions are golden. Serve immediately.

Makes 5 to 6 servings

Tip: This is a great make-ahead party dish.

Chicken and Black Bean Enchiladas

Chicken Stew with Dumplings

Chicken Stew

2 tablespoons vegetable oil
2 cups sliced carrots
1 cup chopped onion
1 large green bell pepper, sliced
½ cup sliced celery
2 cans (about 14 ounces each) fat-free reduced-sodium chicken broth, divided
¼ cup plus 2 tablespoons all-purpose flour
2 pounds boneless skinless chicken breasts, cut into 1-inch pieces
3 medium potatoes, unpeeled and cut into 1-inch pieces
6 ounces mushrooms, halved
¾ cup frozen peas
1 teaspoon dried basil leaves
¾ teaspoon dried rosemary
¼ teaspoon dried tarragon leaves
¾ to 1 teaspoon salt
¼ teaspoon black pepper

Herb Dumplings

2 cups biscuit baking mix
½ teaspoon dried basil leaves
½ teaspoon dried rosemary
¼ teaspoon dried tarragon leaves
⅔ cup reduced-fat (2%) milk

1. For chicken stew, heat oil in 4-quart Dutch oven over medium heat until hot. Add carrots, onion, bell pepper and celery; cook and stir 5 minutes or until onion is tender. Reserve ½ cup broth; stir remaining broth into vegetable mixture; bring to a boil. Mix reserved ½ cup broth and flour; stir into boiling mixture. Boil, stirring constantly, 1 minute or until thickened. Stir in chicken, potatoes, mushrooms, peas and herbs. Reduce heat; simmer, covered, 18 to 20 minutes or until vegetables are almost tender and chicken is no longer pink in center. Add salt and pepper.

2. For Herb Dumplings, combine biscuit mix and herbs in small bowl; stir in milk to form soft dough. Spoon dumpling mixture on top of stew in 8 large spoonfuls. Reduce heat to low. Cook, uncovered, 10 minutes. Cover and cook 10 minutes or until dumplings are tender and toothpick inserted in centers comes out clean. Serve in shallow bowls.

Makes 8 servings

Chicken Stew with Dumpling

Velveeta® Spicy Chicken Spaghetti

Prep Time: 5 minutes
Bake Time: 40 minutes

12 ounces spaghetti, uncooked
4 boneless skinless chicken breast halves (about 1¼ pounds), cut into strips
1 pound (16 ounces) VELVEETA® Pasteurized Prepared Cheese Product, cut up
1 can (10¾ ounces) condensed cream of chicken soup
1 can (10 ounces) diced tomatoes and green chilies, undrained
1 can (4½ ounces) sliced mushrooms, drained
⅓ cup milk

1. Cook pasta as directed on package; drain. Return to same pan.

2. Spray skillet with no stick cooking spray. Add chicken; cook and stir on medium-high heat 4 to 5 minutes or until cooked through. Add VELVEETA, soup, tomatoes and green chilies, mushrooms and milk; stir on low heat until VELVEETA is melted. Add chicken mixture to pasta; toss to coat. Spoon into greased 13×9-inch baking dish.

3. Bake at 350°F for 35 to 40 minutes or until hot. *Makes 6 to 8 servings*

Santa Monica Burgers

1 package (about 1¼ pounds) PERDUE® Fresh Ground Turkey, Ground Turkey Breast Meat or Ground Chicken
4 strips crisp bacon, crumbled
¼ cup chopped tomato
¼ cup chopped onion
1 teaspoon salt
¼ teaspoon ground pepper
4 to 5 sourdough rolls

In mixing bowl, combine turkey, bacon, tomato, onion, salt and pepper. Form into 4 or 5 burgers and grill following package directions. Serve on split, lightly toasted rolls, garnished with Guaco-Mayo (recipe follows), if desired. *Makes 4 servings*

Guaco-Mayo: In food processor or blender, combine 1 small ripe avocado, ½ cup mayonnaise, 2 tablespoons chopped onion, 2 tablespoons lemon juice and 1 pickled jalapeño pepper. Purée; stir in 1 chopped mild chili and ¼ cup chopped tomato.

Velveeta® Spicy Chicken Spaghetti

Turkey Breast with Southwestern Corn Bread Dressing

5 cups coarsely crumbled prepared corn bread
4 English muffins, coarsely crumbled
3 Anaheim chilies,* roasted, peeled, seeded and chopped
1 red bell pepper, roasted, peeled, seeded and chopped
¾ cup pine nuts, toasted
1 tablespoon chopped fresh cilantro
1 tablespoon chopped fresh parsley
1½ teaspoons chopped fresh basil *or* 1 teaspoon dried basil leaves
1½ teaspoons chopped fresh thyme *or* 1 teaspoon dried thyme leaves
1½ teaspoons chopped fresh oregano *or* 1 teaspoon dried oregano leaves
1 pound Italian turkey sausage
3 cups chopped celery
1 cup chopped onions
2 to 4 tablespoons chicken or turkey broth
1 bone-in turkey breast (5 to 6 pounds)
2 tablespoons minced garlic
½ cup chopped fresh cilantro

**Canned mild green chilies may be substituted.*

1. Preheat oven to 325°F. In large bowl combine corn bread, muffins, chilies, bell pepper, pine nuts, 1 tablespoon cilantro, parsley, basil, thyme and oregano; set aside.

2. In large skillet, over medium-high heat, cook and stir turkey sausage, celery and onions 8 to 10 minutes or until sausage is no longer pink and vegetables are tender. Add to cornbread mixture. Add broth if mixture is too dry; set aside.

3. Loosen skin on both sides of turkey breast, being careful not to tear skin, leaving it connected at breast bone. Spread 1 tablespoon garlic under loosened skin over each breast half. Repeat procedure, spreading ¼ cup cilantro over each breast half.

4. Place turkey breast in 13×9×2-inch roasting pan lightly coated with nonstick cooking spray. Spoon half of stuffing mixture under breast cavity. Spoon remaining stuffing into 2-quart casserole lightly coated with nonstick cooking spray; set aside. Roast turkey breast, uncovered, 2 to 2½ hours or until meat thermometer registers 170°F. Bake remaining stuffing, uncovered, during last 45 minutes.

Makes 12 servings

Turkey Breast with Southwestern Corn Bread Dressing

Southwestern Turkey in Chilies and Cream

1 boneless skinless turkey breast, cut into 1-inch pieces
2 tablespoons plus 2 teaspoons flour, divided
1 can (15 ounces) corn, well drained
1 can (4 ounces) diced green chilies, well drained
1 tablespoon butter
½ cup chicken broth
1 clove garlic, minced
1 teaspoon salt
½ teaspoon paprika
¼ teaspoon dried oregano leaves
¼ teaspoon black pepper
½ cup heavy cream
2 tablespoons chopped fresh cilantro
3 cups hot cooked rice or pasta

Slow Cooker Directions

1. Coat turkey pieces with 2 tablespoons flour; set aside. Place corn and green chilies in slow cooker.

2. Melt butter in large nonstick skillet over medium heat. Add turkey pieces; cook and stir 5 minutes or until lightly browned. Place turkey in slow cooker. Add broth, garlic, salt, paprika, oregano and pepper. Cover and cook on LOW 2 hours or until turkey is tender and no longer pink in center.

3. Stir cream and remaining 2 teaspoons flour in small bowl until smooth. Pour mixture into slow cooker. Cover and cook on HIGH 10 minutes or until slightly thickened. Stir in cilantro. Serve over rice. *Makes 6 (1½-cup) servings*

Turkey Roast with Madeira Sauce

1 PERDUE® FIT 'N EASY® Fresh Skinless and Boneless Turkey Breast (1⅓ pounds)
Salt and ground pepper to taste
Dried rosemary
Dried thyme leaves
3 tablespoons butter or margarine, melted, divided
2 tablespoons all-purpose flour
1 can (about 14 ounces) beef broth
¼ cup Madeira wine

Preheat oven to 375°F. Sprinkle turkey breast lightly on both sides with salt, pepper, rosemary and thyme. Place turkey smooth side down. Roll turkey jelly-roll style, starting with long side, into long cylinder shape. Tie with kitchen string in 3 or 4 places to secure. Place turkey roll in small, shallow roasting pan and brush with 1 tablespoon butter. Roast about 30 minutes (20 to 25 minutes per pound) until cooked through and juices run clear when meat is pierced. Remove turkey to warm serving platter.

To prepare sauce, pour off and reserve pan juices. Add remaining 2 tablespoons butter and flour to roasting pan. Cook over medium heat 4 to 5 minutes until deep golden brown, stirring constantly. Gradually stir in reserved pan juices, broth and Madeira. Simmer sauce about 5 minutes until smooth and thickened, stirring frequently.

Cut and discard strings from turkey roast. Serve with wild rice and sauce.

Makes 4 servings

Turkey Tetrazzini with Roasted Red Peppers

Prep and Cook Time: 20 minutes

6 ounces uncooked egg noodles
3 tablespoons butter or margarine
¼ cup all-purpose flour
1 can (about 14 ounces) chicken broth
1 cup whipping cream
2 tablespoons dry sherry
2 cans (6 ounces each) sliced mushrooms, drained
1 jar (7½ ounces) roasted red peppers drained and cut into ½-inch strips
2 cups chopped cooked turkey
1 teaspoon dried Italian seasoning
½ cup grated Parmesan cheese

1. Cook egg noodles in large saucepan according to package directions. Drain well; return noodles to saucepan.

2. While noodles are cooking, melt butter in medium saucepan over medium heat. Add flour and whisk until smooth. Add chicken broth; bring to a boil over high heat. Remove from heat. Gradually add whipping cream and sherry; stir to combine.

3. Add mushrooms and peppers to noodles; toss to combine. Add half the chicken broth mixture to noodle mixture. Combine remaining chicken broth mixture, turkey and Italian seasoning in large bowl.

4. Spoon noodle mixture into serving dish. Make a well in center of noodles and spoon in turkey mixture. Sprinkle cheese over top. *Makes 6 servings*

Turkey Tetrazzini with Roasted Red Peppers

Turkey Meat Loaf

- 1 tablespoon vegetable oil
- ¾ cup chopped onion
- ½ cup chopped celery
- 1 clove garlic, minced
- ⅔ cup reduced-sodium chicken broth or water
- ½ cup bulgur
- ½ cup egg substitute
- 1 tablespoon reduced-sodium soy sauce
- ¼ teaspoon ground cumin
- ¼ teaspoon paprika
- ¼ teaspoon black pepper
- 8 tablespoons chili sauce, divided
- 1 pound ground turkey breast

1. Heat oil in medium skillet. Add onion, celery and garlic. Cook and stir 3 minutes over low heat. Add broth and bulgur. Bring to a boil. Reduce heat to low. Cover and simmer 10 to 15 minutes or until bulgur is tender and all liquid is absorbed. Transfer to large bowl; cool to lukewarm.

2. Preheat oven to 375°F. Stir egg substitute, soy sauce, cumin, paprika and pepper into bulgur. Add 6 tablespoons chili sauce and ground turkey. Stir well until blended.

3. Pat mixture into greased 8½×4½-inch loaf pan. Top with remaining 2 tablespoons chili sauce.

4. Bake meat loaf about 45 minutes or until browned and juices run clear. Drain off drippings. Let stand 10 minutes. Remove from pan. Cut into 10 slices.

Makes 5 servings (2 slices each)

Turkey Meat Loaf

Saucy-Spicy Turkey Meatballs

1 pound ground turkey
⅓ cup dry bread crumbs
1 egg
1 clove garlic, minced
2 tablespoons light soy sauce, divided
1 teaspoon grated fresh ginger
¾ to 1 teaspoon red pepper flakes, divided
1 tablespoon vegetable oil
1 can (20 ounces) pineapple chunks, undrained
2 tablespoons lemon juice or orange juice
2 tablespoons honey
1 tablespoon cornstarch
1 large red bell pepper, seeded and cut into 1-inch triangles
Hot cooked rice

1. Combine turkey, bread crumbs, egg, garlic, 1 tablespoon soy sauce, ginger and ½ teaspoon red pepper flakes in large bowl. Shape turkey mixture into 1-inch meatballs.

2. Heat oil in wok or large skillet over medium-high heat. Add meatballs and cook 4 to 5 minutes or until no longer pink in centers, turning to brown all sides. Remove from wok; set aside.

3. Drain pineapple, reserving juice. Add enough water to juice to make 1 cup liquid. Whisk together pineapple juice mixture, lemon juice, honey, cornstarch, remaining 1 tablespoon soy sauce and ¼ teaspoon red pepper flakes. Pour into wok. Cook and stir over medium-high heat until sauce thickens.

4. Add meatballs, pineapple and bell pepper to sauce. Cook and stir until hot. Adjust seasoning with remaining ¼ teaspoon hot pepper flakes, if desired. Serve over rice.

Makes 4 to 5 servings

Saucy-Spicy Turkey Meatballs

Roast Turkey Breast with Spinach-Blue Cheese Stuffing

1 frozen boneless turkey breast, thawed (3½ to 4 pounds)
1 package (10 ounces) frozen chopped spinach, thawed and squeezed dry
2 ounces blue cheese or feta cheese
2 ounces reduced-fat cream cheese
½ cup finely chopped green onions
4½ teaspoons Dijon mustard
4½ teaspoons dried basil leaves
2 teaspoons dried oregano leaves
Black pepper to taste
Paprika

1. Preheat oven to 350°F. Coat roasting pan and rack with nonstick cooking spray.

2. Unroll turkey breast, rinse and pat dry. Place between 2 sheets of plastic wrap. Pound turkey breast with flat side of meat mallet to create even piece about 1 inch thick. Remove and discard skin from one side of turkey breast; turn meat over so skin side faces down.

3. Combine spinach, blue cheese, cream cheese, green onions, mustard, basil and oregano in medium bowl; mix well. Spread evenly over turkey breast. Roll up turkey so skin is on top.

4. Carefully place turkey breast on rack; sprinkle with pepper and paprika. Roast 1½ hours or until no longer pink in center of breast. Remove from oven and let stand 10 minutes before removing skin and slicing. Cut into ¼-inch slices.

Makes 14 servings

Roast Turkey Breast with Spinach-Blue Cheese Stuffing

Mama's Best Ever Spaghetti & Meatballs

Prep Time: 10 minutes
Cook Time: 20 minutes

1 pound lean ground beef
½ cup Italian seasoned dry bread crumbs
1 egg
1 jar (26 to 28 ounces) RAGÚ® Old World Style® Pasta Sauce
8 ounces spaghetti, cooked and drained

1. In medium bowl, combine ground beef, bread crumbs and egg; shape into 12 meatballs.

2. In 3-quart saucepan, bring Ragú Pasta Sauce to a boil over medium-high heat. Gently stir in meatballs.

3. Reduce heat to low and simmer covered, stirring occasionally, 20 minutes or until meatballs are no longer pink in centers. Serve over hot spaghetti; sprinkle with shredded Parmesan cheese; if desired. *Makes 4 servings*

Mama's Best Ever Spaghetti & Meatballs

Steak Diane

2 large well-trimmed boneless beef top loin steaks, 1 inch thick, cut in half crosswise *or* 1 boneless beef top sirloin steak (about 1¼ pounds total), cut into 4 serving pieces
½ teaspoon black pepper, divided
3 tablespoons butter, divided
2 tablespoons Dijon mustard
2 tablespoons Worcestershire sauce
½ cup chopped shallots or sweet onion
8 ounces fresh oyster mushrooms, cut in half or 8 ounces cremini mushrooms, sliced
2 tablespoons brandy or Cognac
⅔ cup heavy cream
1½ teaspoons chopped fresh thyme *or* ½ teaspoon dried thyme leaves, crushed
4 Baked potatoes (optional)
Basil flowers and geranium leaves for garnish

1. Sprinkle steaks with ¼ teaspoon pepper. Melt 1 tablespoon butter in large skillet over medium-high heat. Add steaks. Cook 2 minutes per side or until browned. Reduce heat to medium; cook 3 to 4 minutes more per side for medium-rare or to desired doneness.

2. Transfer steaks to large shallow dish; spread mustard over both sides of steaks. Spoon Worcestershire sauce over steaks.

3. Melt remaining 2 tablespoons butter in same skillet over medium heat. Add shallots; cook and stir 4 minutes. Add mushrooms; cook 5 minutes or until mushrooms are softened. Add brandy to skillet; carefully ignite brandy with lighted long match or barbecue starter flame. Let flames burn off alcohol 30 seconds or until flames subside.

4. Stir in cream, thyme and remaining ¼ teaspoon pepper. Cook about 3 minutes or until sauce thickens. Return steaks and liquid to skillet. Cook 3 minutes or until heated through, turning once. Spoon sauce over steaks. Serve steaks with baked potatoes. Garnish, if desired.

Makes 4 servings

Steak Diane

Swedish Meatballs

1½ cups fresh bread crumbs
1 cup (½ pint) heavy cream
2 tablespoons butter or margarine, divided
1 small onion, chopped
1 pound ground beef
½ pound ground pork
3 tablespoons chopped fresh parsley, divided
1½ teaspoons salt
¼ teaspoon black pepper
¼ teaspoon ground allspice
1 cup beef broth
1 cup sour cream
1 tablespoon all-purpose flour

Combine bread crumbs and cream in small bowl; mix well. Let stand 10 minutes. Melt 1 tablespoon butter in large skillet over medium heat. Add onion. Cook and stir 5 minutes or until onion is tender. Combine beef, pork, bread crumb mixture, onion, 2 tablespoons parsley, salt, pepper and allspice in large bowl; mix well. Cover; refrigerate 1 hour.

Pat meat mixture into 1-inch-thick square on cutting board. Cut into 36 squares. Shape each square into a ball. Melt remaining 1 tablespoon butter in same large skillet over medium heat. Add meatballs. Cook 10 minutes or until browned on all sides and no longer pink in centers. Remove meatballs from skillet; drain on paper towels.

Drain drippings from skillet; discard. Pour broth into skillet. Heat over medium-high heat, stirring frequently and scraping up any browned bits. Reduce heat to low.

Combine sour cream and flour in small bowl; mix well. Stir sour cream mixture into skillet. Cook 5 minutes, stirring constantly. *Do not boil.* Add meatballs. Cook 5 minutes more. Sprinkle with remaining 1 tablespoon parsley. Garnish as desired.

Makes 5 to 6 servings

Swedish Meatballs

Beef and Vegetables in Rich Burgundy Sauce

1 package (8 ounces) sliced mushrooms
1 package (8 ounces) baby carrots
1 medium green bell pepper, cut into thin strips
1 boneless beef chuck roast (2½ pounds)
1 can (10½ ounces) condensed golden mushroom soup
¼ cup dry red wine or beef broth
1 tablespoon Worcestershire sauce
1 package (1 ounce) dry onion soup mix
¼ teaspoon black pepper
2 tablespoons water
3 tablespoons cornstarch
4 cups hot cooked noodles
Chopped fresh parsley (optional)

Slow Cooker Directions

1. Place mushrooms, carrots and bell pepper in slow cooker. Place roast on top of vegetables. Combine mushroom soup, wine, Worcestershire sauce, soup mix and black pepper in medium bowl; mix well. Pour soup mixture over roast. Cover and cook on LOW 8 to 10 hours.

2. Blend water into cornstarch in cup until smooth; set aside. Transfer roast to cutting board; cover with foil. Let stand 10 to 15 minutes before slicing.

3. Turn slow cooker to HIGH. Stir cornstarch mixture into vegetable mixture; cover and cook 10 minutes or until thickened. Serve over cooked noodles. Garnish with parsley, if desired.

Makes 6 to 8 servings

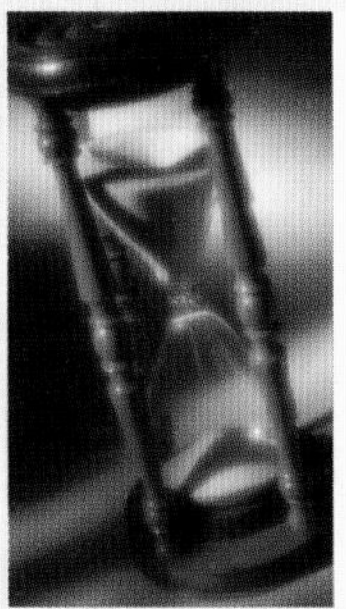

Quick Tip

For even cooking, layer ingredients in a slow cooker in the order given in the recipe. The slow cooker can take as long as 20 minutes to regain heat lost when it is uncovered, so keep the lid on!

Beef and Vegetables in Rich Burgundy Sauce

Lasagna Supreme

8 ounces uncooked lasagna noodles
½ pound ground beef
½ pound mild Italian sausage, casings removed
1 medium onion, chopped
2 cloves garlic, minced
1 can (14½ ounces) whole peeled tomatoes, undrained and chopped
1 can (6 ounces) tomato paste
2 teaspoons dried basil leaves
1 teaspoon dried marjoram leaves
1 can (4 ounces) sliced mushrooms, drained
2 eggs
2 cups (16 ounces) cream-style cottage cheese
¾ cup grated Parmesan cheese, divided
2 tablespoons dried parsley flakes
½ teaspoon salt
½ teaspoon black pepper
2 cups (8 ounces) shredded Cheddar cheese
3 cups (12 ounces) shredded mozzarella cheese

1. Cook lasagna noodles according to package directions; drain.

2. Cook meats, onion and garlic in large skillet over medium-high heat until meat is brown, stirring to separate meat. Drain drippings from skillet.

3. Add tomatoes with juice, tomato paste, basil and marjoram. Reduce heat to low. Cover; simmer 15 minutes, stirring often. Stir in mushrooms; set aside.

4. Preheat oven to 375°F. Beat eggs in large bowl; add cottage cheese, ½ cup Parmesan cheese, parsley, salt and pepper. Mix well.

5. Place half the noodles in bottom of greased 13×9-inch baking pan. Spread half the cottage cheese mixture over noodles, then half the meat mixture and half the Cheddar cheese and mozzarella cheese. Repeat layers. Sprinkle with remaining ¼ cup Parmesan cheese.

6. Bake lasagna 40 to 45 minutes or until bubbly. Let stand 10 minutes before cutting.

Makes 8 to 10 servings

Note: Lasagna may be assembled, covered and refrigerated up to 2 days in advance. Bake, uncovered, in preheated 375°F oven 60 minutes or until bubbly.

Beef Barley Soup

Nonstick cooking spray
¾ pound boneless beef top round, excess fat trimmed, cut into ½-inch pieces
3 cans (about 14 ounces each) beef broth
1 can (14½ ounces) no-salt-added diced tomatoes
2 cups ½-inch unpeeled potato cubes
1½ cups ½-inch green bean slices
1 cup chopped onion
1 cup sliced carrots
½ cup pearled barley
1 tablespoon cider vinegar
2 teaspoons caraway seeds, lightly crushed
2 teaspoons dried marjoram leaves, crushed
2 teaspoons dried thyme leaves, crushed
½ teaspoon salt
½ teaspoon black pepper

Coat large saucepan with cooking spray; heat over medium heat. Add beef; cook and stir until browned on all sides. Add beef broth, tomatoes with liquid, potatoes, green beans, onion, carrots, barley, vinegar, caraway seeds, marjoram, thyme, salt and pepper; bring to a boil over high heat. Reduce heat to low. Simmer, covered, about 2 hours or until beef is fork-tender, uncovering saucepan during last 30 minutes of cooking.

Makes 4 servings

Roasted Herb & Garlic Tenderloin

1 well-trimmed beef tenderloin roast (3 to 4 pounds)
1 tablespoon black peppercorns
2 tablespoons chopped fresh basil *or* 2 teaspoons dried basil leaves
4½ teaspoons chopped fresh thyme *or* 1½ teaspoons dried thyme leaves
1 tablespoon chopped fresh rosemary *or* 1 teaspoon dried rosemary
1 tablespoon minced garlic
Salt and black pepper (optional)

1. Preheat oven to 425°F. To hold shape of roast, tie roast with cotton string at 1½-inch intervals. Place roast on meat rack in shallow roasting pan.

2. Place peppercorns in small heavy resealable plastic food storage bag. Squeeze out excess air; seal bag tightly. Pound peppercorns with flat side of meat mallet or rolling pin until peppercorns are cracked.

3. Combine cracked peppercorns, basil, thyme, rosemary and garlic in small bowl; rub over top surface of roast.

4. Roast 40 to 50 minutes for medium or until internal temperatures reaches 145°F when tested with meat thermometer inserted into the thickest part of roast.

5. Transfer roast to cutting board; cover with foil. Let stand 10 to 15 minutes before carving. Internal temperature will continue to rise 5 to 10°F during stand time. Remove and discard string. To serve, carve crosswise into ½-inch-thick slices with large carving knife. Season with salt and pepper. *Makes 10 to 12 servings*

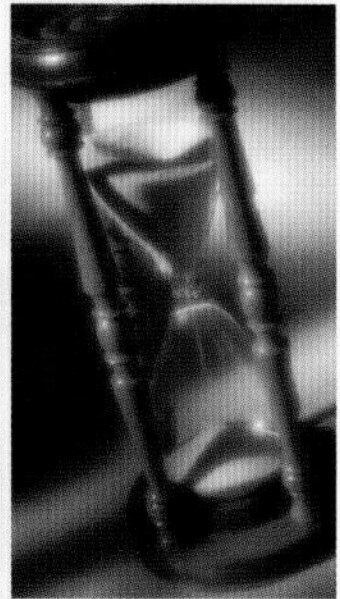

Quick Tip

To save time when preparing this recipe, substitute purchased cracked peppercorns and eliminate step 2. Placing a roast on a meat rack allows heat to circulate underneath and results in more even roasting.

Roasted Herb & Garlic Tenderloin

Pot Roast Carbonnade

- 6 thick slices applewood or other smoked bacon (about 6 ounces)
- 2 tablespoons all-purpose flour
- ¾ teaspoon salt
- ½ teaspoon black pepper
- 1 well-trimmed round bone* beef chuck pot roast (about 3½ pounds)
- 3 large Spanish onions (about 2 pounds), thinly sliced
- 2 tablespoons light brown sugar
- 1 can (about 14 ounces) beef broth
- 1 bottle (12 ounces) beer (not dark)
- 2 teaspoons dried thyme leaves
- 2 bay leaves
- Boiled potatoes or hot cooked egg noodles (optional)

**A well-trimmed, 3-pound boneless beef chuck pot roast may be substituted; however, the bone in the pot roast will give the sauce more flavor.*

1. Preheat oven to 350°F. Cook bacon in Dutch oven over medium heat until crisp. Transfer bacon to paper towel with tongs, reserving drippings in Dutch oven. Crumble bacon; set aside.

2. Combine flour, salt and pepper on large plate. Place pot roast on flour mixture; roll to coat well. Place pot roast in drippings in Dutch oven. Brown over medium-low heat about 4 to 5 minutes per side; remove to platter. Set aside.

3. Pour off all but 2 tablespoons drippings from Dutch oven. Add onions to drippings; cover and cook 10 minutes over medium heat, stirring once. Uncover; sprinkle with sugar. Cook, uncovered, over medium-high heat 10 minutes or until golden, stirring frequently.

4. Add broth, beer, thyme and bay leaves to Dutch oven; bring to a boil. Return pot roast with any accumulated juices to Dutch oven. Remove from heat; spoon sauce over top. Cover and bake 2 to 2¼ hours until meat is fork-tender.

5. Transfer meat to carving board; tent with foil.

6. Remove bay leaves; discard. Skim fat from juices with large spoon; discard. Place ½ of juice mixture in food processor; process until smooth. Repeat with remaining juice mixture; return puréed mixture to Dutch oven. Stir reserved bacon into sauce; cook over medium heat until heated through.

7. Discard bone from roast; carve roast into ¼-inch-thick slices with large carving knife. Spoon sauce over roast. Serve with boiled potatoes. *Makes 8 servings*

Pot Roast Carbonnade

Mustard Crusted Rib Roast

1 (3-rib) standing beef rib roast, trimmed* (6 to 7 pounds)
3 tablespoons Dijon mustard
1 tablespoon plus 1½ teaspoons chopped fresh tarragon *or* 1½ teaspoons dried tarragon leaves
3 cloves garlic, minced
¼ cup dry red wine
⅓ cup finely chopped shallots (about 2 shallots)
1 tablespoon all-purpose flour
1 cup beef broth
Mashed potatoes (optional)
Fresh tarragon sprigs for garnish

**Ask meat retailer to remove chine bone for easier carving. Trim fat to ¼-inch thickness.*

1. Preheat oven to 450°F. Place roast, bone side down, in shallow roasting pan. Combine mustard, chopped tarragon and garlic in small bowl; spread over all surfaces of roast, except bottom. Insert meat thermometer into thickest part of roast, not touching bone or fat. Roast 10 minutes.

2. *Reduce oven temperature to 325°F.* Roast about 20 minutes per pound for medium or until internal temperature reaches 145°F.

3. Transfer roast to cutting board; cover with foil. Let stand 10 to 15 minutes before carving. Internal temperature will continue to rise 5° to 10°F during stand time.

4. To make gravy, pour fat from roasting pan, reserving 1 tablespoon in medium saucepan. Add wine to roasting pan; place over 2 burners. Cook over medium heat 2 minutes or until slightly thickened, stirring to scrape up browned bits; reserve.

5. Add shallots to reserved drippings in saucepan; cook and stir over medium heat 4 minutes or until softened. Add flour; cook and stir 1 minute. Add broth and reserved wine mixture; cook 5 minutes or until sauce thickens, stirring occasionally. Pour through strainer into gravy boat, pressing with back of spoon on shallots; discard solids.

6. Carve roast into ½-inch-thick slices. Serve with mashed potatoes and gravy. Garnish, if desired.

Makes 6 to 8 servings

Mustard Crusted Rib Roast

Beef Stroganoff

Prep and Cook Time: 20 minutes

12 ounces uncooked wide egg noodles
1 can (10¾ ounces) condensed cream of mushroom soup
1 cup (8 ounces) sour cream
1 package (1¼ ounces) dry onion soup mix
1¼ to 1½ pounds lean ground beef
½ (10-ounce) package frozen peas, thawed

1. Place 3 quarts water in 8-quart stockpot; bring to a boil over high heat. Stir in noodles; boil, uncovered, 6 minutes or until tender. Drain.

2. Meanwhile, place mushroom soup, sour cream and onion soup mix in medium bowl. Stir until blended; set aside. Brown meat in large skillet over high heat 6 to 8 minutes or until meat is no longer pink, stirring to separate meat. Pour off drippings. Reduce heat to low. Add soup mixture; stir over low heat until bubbly. Stir in peas; heat through. Serve over noodles. *Makes 6 servings*

Serving Suggestion: Serve with tossed green salad or fresh fruit.

Manwich Meatloaf

1 can (15.5 ounces) HUNT'S® Manwich Original Sloppy Joe Sauce, divided
1 pound ground beef
¾ cup quick-cooking oats
2 eggs

In large bowl, combine ½ can Manwich Sauce, ground beef, oats and eggs; mix well. Press into loaf pan. Bake at 350°F for 30 minutes; drain off drippings from pan.

Pour remaining ½ can Manwich Sauce evenly over meatloaf. Bake at 350°F 30 minutes. *Makes 4 to 6 servings*

Cheeseburger Macaroni Stew

Prep Time: 5 minutes
Cook Time: 15 minutes

1 pound ground beef
1 can (28 ounces) crushed tomatoes in purée
1½ cups uncooked elbow macaroni
2 tablespoons *French's*® Worcestershire Sauce
1 cup shredded Cheddar cheese
1½ cups *French's*® French Fried Onions

1. Cook meat in large nonstick skillet over medium-high heat until browned and no longer pink; drain.

2. Add tomatoes, macaroni and *1½ cups water*. Bring to boiling. Boil, partially covered, 10 minutes until macaroni is tender. Stir in Worcestershire.

3. Sprinkle with cheese and French Fried Onions.

Makes 6 servings

Tip: For a Southwestern flavor, add 2 tablespoons chili powder to ground beef and substitute 2 tablespoons ***Frank's***® RedHot Sauce for the Worcestershire.

Ragú® Chili Mac

Prep Time: 10 minutes
Cook Time: 25 minutes

1 tablespoon olive or vegetable oil
1 medium green bell pepper, chopped
1 pound ground beef
1 jar (26 to 28 ounces) RAGÚ® Old World Style® Pasta Sauce
2 tablespoons chili powder
8 ounces elbow macaroni, cooked and drained

1. In 12-inch nonstick skillet, heat oil over medium-high heat and cook green bell pepper, stirring occasionally, 3 minutes. Add ground beef and brown, stirring occasionally; drain.

2. Stir in Ragú Pasta Sauce and chili powder. Bring to a boil over high heat. Reduce heat to low and simmer covered 10 minutes.

3. Stir in macaroni and heat through. Serve, if desired, with sour cream and shredded Cheddar cheese.

Makes 4 servings

Ragú® Chili Mac

Tenderloins with Roasted Garlic Sauce

2 whole garlic bulbs, separated but not peeled (about 5 ounces)
⅔ cup A.1.® Steak Sauce, divided
¼ cup dry red wine
¼ cup finely chopped onion
4 (4- to 6-ounce) beef tenderloin steaks, about 1 inch thick

Place unpeeled garlic cloves on baking sheet. Bake at 500°F for 15 to 20 minutes or until garlic is soft; cool. Squeeze garlic pulp from skins; chop pulp slightly. In small saucepan, combine garlic pulp, ½ cup steak sauce, wine and onion. Heat to a boil; reduce heat and simmer for 5 minutes. Keep warm.

Grill steaks over medium heat for 5 minutes on each side or until done, brushing with remaining steak sauce. Serve with garlic sauce. *Makes 4 servings*

Easy Beef Lasagna

Prep Time: 30 minutes
Cook Time: 35 minutes

1 pound ground beef
1 jar (26 to 28 ounces) RAGÚ® Old World Style® Pasta Sauce
1 container (15 ounces) ricotta cheese
2 cups shredded mozzarella cheese (about 8 ounces)
½ cup grated Parmesan cheese
2 eggs
12 lasagna noodles, cooked and drained

1. Preheat oven to 375°F. In 12-inch skillet, brown ground beef; drain. Stir in Ragú Pasta Sauce; heat through.

2. In large bowl, combine ricotta cheese, mozzarella cheese, ¼ cup Parmesan cheese and eggs.

3. In 13×9-inch baking dish, evenly spread 1 cup meat sauce. Arrange 4 lasagna noodles lengthwise over sauce, then 1 cup meat sauce and ½ of the ricotta cheese mixture; repeat, ending with sauce. Cover with aluminum foil and bake 30 minutes. Sprinkle with remaining ¼ cup Parmesan cheese. Bake uncovered 5 minutes. Let stand 10 minutes before serving. *Makes 10 servings*

Tenderloin with Roasted Garlic Sauce

Mediterranean Microwave Meat Loaf

Prep and Cook Time: 20 minutes

- **1 pound lean ground beef**
- **¼ pound Italian sausage, casings removed**
- **½ cup dry bread crumbs**
- **¼ cup grated Parmesan cheese**
- **1 large egg**
- **⅓ cup plus 2 tablespoons prepared pasta sauce, divided**
- **2 tablespoons lemon juice, divided**
- **½ teaspoon ground allspice**
- **¼ teaspoon black pepper**

Microwave Directions

1. In large bowl combine ground beef, sausage, bread crumbs, cheese, egg, ⅓ cup pasta sauce, 1 tablespoon lemon juice, allspice and pepper. Mix until blended. Pat into ball. Place in 9-inch glass pie plate or shallow microwavable casserole 9 to 10 inches in diameter. Press into 7-inch circle.

2. Microwave, lightly covered with paper towels, at HIGH (100%) 8 minutes. Pour off drippings. Meanwhile combine 2 tablespoons pasta sauce and remaining 1 tablespoon lemon juice; spread over top of meat loaf. Microwave 3 to 5 minutes more or until instant-read thermometer registers 160°F in center. Let stand 5 minutes before serving.

Makes 4 servings

Serving Suggestion: Serve with frozen stuffed potatoes heated according to package directions and tossed green salad.

Mediterranean Microwave Meat Loaf

Apricot Pork Chops and Dressing

- **1 box (6 ounces) herb-seasoned stuffing mix**
- **½ cup dried apricots (about 16), cut into quarters**
- **6 sheets (18×12-inches) heavy-duty foil, lightly sprayed with nonstick cooking spray**
- **6 bone-in pork chops, ½ inch thick**
- **Salt**
- **Black pepper**
- **6 tablespoons apricot jam**
- **1 bag (16 ounces) frozen green peas**
- **3 cups matchstick carrots***

**Precut matchstick carrots are available in the produce section of large supermarkets.*

1. Preheat oven to 450°F. Prepare stuffing mix according to package directions; stir in apricots.

2. Place ½ cup stuffing mixture in center of one sheet of foil. Place 1 pork chop on stuffing mixture, pressing down slightly and shaping stuffing to conform to shape of chop. Sprinkle chop with salt and pepper. Spread 1 tablespoon apricot jam over pork chop.

3. Place ⅔ cup peas beside pork chop in curve of bone. Arrange ½ cup carrots around outside of chop.

4. Double fold sides and ends of foil to seal packet, leaving head space for heat circulation. Repeat with remaining stuffing mixture, pork chops, salt, pepper, jam and vegetables to make 5 more packets. Place packets on baking sheet.

5. Bake 25 to 26 minutes or until pork chops are barely pink in center and vegetables are tender. Remove from oven. Carefully open one end of each packet to allow steam to escape. Open packets and transfer contents to serving plates.

Makes 6 servings

Apricot Pork Chop and Dressing

Italian Pork Chops

2 cups uncooked long-grain white rice
4 large pork chops (½ inch thick)
1 teaspoon basil, crushed
1 can (26 ounces) DEL MONTE® Spaghetti Sauce with Mushrooms or Chunky Italian Herb Spaghetti Sauce
1 green bell pepper, cut into thin strips

1. Cook rice according to package directions.

2. Preheat broiler. Sprinkle meat with basil; season with salt and black pepper, if desired. Place meat on broiler pan. Broil 4 inches from heat about 6 minutes on each side or until no longer pink in center.

3. Combine sauce and green pepper in microwavable dish. Cover with plastic wrap; slit to vent. Microwave on HIGH 5 to 6 minutes or until green pepper is tender-crisp and sauce is heated through. Add meat; cover with sauce. Microwave 1 minute. Serve over hot rice. *Makes 4 servings*

Serving Suggestion: Serve with boiled potatoes and vegetables.

Onion-Baked Pork Chops

Prep Time: 5 minutes
Cook Time: 20 minutes

1 envelope LIPTON® RECIPE SECRETS® Onion Soup Mix*
⅓ cup plain dry bread crumbs
4 bone-in pork chops, 1 inch thick
1 egg, well beaten

**Also terrific with LIPTON RECIPE SECRETS Golden Onion or Savory Herb with Garlic Soup Mix.*

1. Preheat oven to 400°F. In small bowl, combine soup mix and bread crumbs. Dip chops in egg, then bread crumb mixture until evenly coated.

2. On baking sheet, arrange chops.

3. Bake uncovered 20 minutes or until barely pink in center. *Makes 4 servings*

Italian Pork Chop

Skillet Pork Chops with Maple Apples

Prep and Cook Time: 26 minutes

1 package (12 ounces) uncooked egg noodles
1 teaspoon dried oregano leaves
1 teaspoon dried thyme leaves
½ teaspoon salt
½ teaspoon ground nutmeg
¼ teaspoon black pepper
4 well-trimmed center-cut pork chops, cut ½ inch thick
2 tablespoons margarine or butter, divided
1 red apple
¼ cup maple syrup
2 tablespoons lemon juice
½ teaspoon ground ginger

1. Prepare noodles according to package directions; drain.

2. While noodles are cooking, combine oregano, thyme, salt, nutmeg and pepper in small bowl; sprinkle over pork chops.

3. Heat 1 tablespoon margarine in large skillet until hot. Add pork chops and cook over medium heat 5 to 7 minutes per side or until pork is barely pink in center. Remove from skillet and cover to keep warm.

4. Cut apple in half; core and cut into slices. Add remaining 1 tablespoon margarine and apple to skillet. Cook, stirring occasionally, about 3 minutes or until tender. Stir in syrup, lemon juice, ginger and additional salt and pepper to taste. Cook about 2 minutes or until slightly thickened.

5. Serve pork chops and apple mixture over noodles. *Makes 4 servings*

Skillet Pork Chop with Maple Apples

Pilaf-Stuffed Pork Loin Roast

5 tablespoons butter or margarine, divided
¼ cup chopped onion
¼ cup chopped celery
1 clove garlic, minced
2 cups chicken broth
1 cup uncooked long grain and wild rice blend
½ cup finely chopped pecans, toasted*
3 tablespoons orange marmalade
4 teaspoons dried thyme leaves, divided
¾ teaspoon salt
½ teaspoon black pepper
1 boneless, rolled and tied pork loin roast (5 to 6 pounds)**
1 onion, sliced and separated into rings
½ cup water
1 tablespoon vegetable oil
2 tablespoons soy sauce
Orange juice
2 tablespoons all-purpose flour
Plum slices and fresh chervil for garnish

**To toast pecans, spread in single layer on baking sheet. Bake in preheated 350°F oven 6 to 8 minutes or until lightly browned, stirring often.*

***Ask your meat retailer to try and keep the roast in 1 piece when boning.*

1. Preheat oven to 325°F. Melt 2 tablespoons butter in medium saucepan over medium heat; stir in chopped onion, celery and garlic. Cook until onion is tender, stirring frequently. Add broth; bring to a boil. Stir in rice blend. Reduce heat to low; cover and simmer 20 minutes. Remove from heat; let stand 5 minutes or until all liquid is absorbed.

2. Add pecans, marmalade, 1 teaspoon thyme, salt and pepper to rice blend; toss gently until blended. Cover; set aside.

3. Cut and remove strings from roast; discard. To butterfly roast, split roast in half where the 2 pieces fall apart. (If possible, keep roast in 1 piece.)

4. To butterfly each roast half, make horizontal cut starting from center crease of roast to within 1 inch of opposite edge. (If roast is in 2 pieces, butterfly 1 piece through center.) Open roast half and press uncut edge to flatten as much as possible.

continued on page 80

Pilaf-Stuffed Pork Loin Roast

Pilaf-Stuffed Pork Loin Roast, continued

5. Butterfly remaining roast half, starting from center crease and cutting to but not through outside edge. Open both sides of roast to obtain 1 piece with four sections of uniform thickness. (If roast is in 2 pieces, secure with wooden picks.)

6. Spoon rice mixture over roast, leaving 1-inch border. Cut enough heavy cotton string to tie roast at 1-inch intervals, making sure strings are long enough to tie securely. Place strings under roast. Beginning with 1 long side, roll roast jelly-roll fashion and tie with strings, being careful to keep 2 pieces together if necessary. Tie entire roast lengthwise with additional string.

7. Arrange onion rings in single layer in greased shallow roasting pan. Pour water over onion rings. Place meat rack in roasting pan. Place roast on rack; brush with oil and sprinkle with remaining 3 teaspoons thyme. Insert meat thermometer into thickest part of roast but not in rice stuffing.

8. Cover with foil; roast in oven 2½ hours or until until internal temperature reaches 165°F when tested with meat thermometer.

9. Transfer roast to cutting board; cover with foil. Let stand 10 to 15 minutes before carving. Internal temperature will rise 5° to 10°F during stand time. Remove onion rings from roasting pan; discard. Meanwhile, to deglaze pan, pour soy sauce into pan drippings. Cook over medium-high heat, scraping up any browned bits and stirring frequently. Transfer mixture to deglazing measuring cup; let stand until fat rises to surface. Pour mixture into 2- or 4-cup measuring cup, stopping short of risen fat. (If deglazing measuring cup is unavailable, spoon fat from surface.) Add orange juice to measuring cup to equal 1¼ cups; set aside.

10. Melt remaining 3 tablespoons butter in small saucepan over medium heat; add flour, stirring until blended with wire whisk. Add orange juice mixture; cook until thickened and bubbly, whisking frequently. Season with additional salt and black pepper, if desired.

11. Remove strings from roast; discard. Carve roast and serve with orange sauce. Garnish, if desired.

Makes 12 servings

Roast Pork Loin Southwest Style

Prep Time: 15 minutes
Cook Time: 1½ hours

- **1 (4-pound) boneless pork loin roast, trimmed**
- **1 tablespoon olive oil**
- **2 medium tomatoes, chopped and seeded (about 2 cups)**
- **1 medium onion, chopped (about 1 cup)**
- **½ cup chopped fresh cilantro**
- **1 tomatillo, peeled, chopped (about ⅓ cup) (optional)**
- **4 cloves garlic, minced**
- **1 jalapeño pepper,* seeded, chopped (optional)**
- **1 can (4 ounces) chopped green chilies, drained**
- **½ teaspoon dried oregano leaves**
- **½ teaspoon ground cumin**
- **½ teaspoon ground red pepper**
- **½ teaspoon ground coriander**

**Jalapeño peppers can sting and irritate the skin; wear rubber gloves when handling peppers and do not touch eyes. Wash hands after handling.*

Heat oil in large skillet over medium heat. Add tomatoes, onion, cilantro, tomatillo, garlic, jalapeño pepper and chilies; cook about 2 minutes or until onion is tender, stirring frequently. Add oregano, cumin, red pepper and coriander; mix well. Refrigerate mixture until thoroughly chilled.

Heat oven to 325°F. Spray shallow baking pan with nonstick cooking spray. Using sharp knife, cut 8 to 10 slits about 1 inch long and 1 inch deep into top and sides of pork roast. Press heaping teaspoonful of cold vegetable mixture into each slit; spread remaining mixture over top and sides of roast. Place in prepared pan. Roast about 1½ hours, or until meat thermometer registers 155°F. Let stand 10 minutes before slicing.

Makes 16 servings

Favorite recipe from *National Pork Board*

Roast Pork with Tart Cherries

1 boneless rolled pork roast (3½ to 4 pounds)
3 teaspoons bottled grated horseradish, divided
1 teaspoon ground coriander
½ teaspoon black pepper
1 can (16 ounces) pitted tart cherries, undrained
½ cup chicken broth
⅓ cup Madeira wine or dry sherry
1 tablespoon brown sugar
1 tablespoon Dijon mustard
⅛ teaspoon ground cloves
4 teaspoons grated orange peel
Orange peel twist (optional)

1. Preheat oven to 400°F. Place pork on meat rack in shallow roasting pan. Insert meat thermometer into thickest part of roast.

2. Combine 2 teaspoons horseradish, coriander and pepper in small bowl. Rub over pork. Roast pork 10 minutes; remove from oven. *Reduce oven temperature to 350°F.*

3. Add cherries with juice and broth to pan. Cover pan loosely with foil. Roast about 1 hour 30 minutes, basting every 20 minutes, or until internal temperature of roast reaches 165°F when tested with meat thermometer inserted into the thickest part of roast. (Cook, uncovered, during last 20 minutes).

4. Transfer pork to cutting board; cover with foil. Let stand 10 to 15 minutes before carving. Internal temperature will continue to rise 5° to 10°F during stand time.

5. Meanwhile, remove meat rack from roasting pan. Pour contents of pan through strainer into small saucepan, reserving cherries. Stir wine, sugar, mustard, remaining 1 teaspoon horseradish, cloves and grated orange peel into saucepan. Bring to a boil over medium-high heat. Boil 10 minutes or until sauce is thickened. Stir in reserved cherries.

6. Carve pork into thin slices; place on serving platter. Pour some cherry sauce around pork. Serve with remaining cherry sauce. Garnish with orange peel twist, if desired.

Makes 8 servings

Roasted Pork with Tart Cherries

Italian-Glazed Pork Chops

Prep Time: 10 minutes
Cook Time: 25 minutes

1 tablespoon olive or vegetable oil
8 bone-in pork chops
1 medium zucchini, thinly sliced
1 medium red bell pepper, chopped
1 medium onion, thinly sliced
3 cloves garlic, finely chopped
¼ cup dry red wine or beef broth
1 jar (26 to 28 ounces) RAGÚ® Chunky Gardenstyle Pasta Sauce

1. In 12-inch skillet, heat oil over medium-high heat and brown chops. Remove chops and set aside.

2. In same skillet, cook zucchini, red bell pepper, onion and garlic, stirring occasionally, 4 minutes. Stir in wine and Ragú Pasta Sauce.

3. Return chops to skillet, turning to coat with sauce. Simmer covered 15 minutes or until chops are tender and barely pink in center. Serve, if desired, over hot cooked couscous or rice. *Makes 8 servings*

Stuffed Pork Roast

1 boneless pork roast, about 4 to 5 pounds
1 teaspoon LAWRY'S® Garlic Salt
¼ cup butter
1 cup diced onion
1 cup diced celery
½ cup fresh bread crumbs
1 package (1.50 ounces) LAWRY'S® Spices & Seasonings for Pot Roast

Sprinkle roast cavity with Garlic Salt. In medium skillet, heat butter. Add onion and celery and cook over medium-high heat until tender. Add bread crumbs; mix well. Fill roast cavity with stuffing. Rub roast thoroughly with Spices & Seasonings for Pot Roast. Place on rack in roasting pan. Roast, uncovered, in 400°F oven 30 minutes. *Reduce heat to 350°F* and continue roasting approximately 30 minutes per pound or until internal temperature reaches 185°F. *Makes 8 servings*

Italian-Glazed Pork Chop

Cheesy Broccoli Bake

1 (10-ounce) package frozen chopped broccoli
1 (10¾-ounce) can condensed Cheddar cheese soup
½ cup sour cream
2 cups (12 ounces) chopped CURE 81® ham
2 cups cooked rice
½ cup soft torn bread crumbs
1 tablespoon butter or margarine, melted

Heat oven to 350°F. Cook broccoli according to package directions; drain. Combine soup and sour cream. Stir in broccoli, ham and rice. Spoon into 1½-quart casserole. Combine bread crumbs and butter; sprinkle over casserole. Bake 30 to 35 minutes or until thoroughly heated. *Makes 4 to 6 servings*

Cheesy Ham Casserole

Prep Time: 15 minutes
Cook Time: 30 minutes

2 cups fresh or frozen broccoli flowerets, thawed
1½ cups KRAFT® Shredded Sharp Cheddar Cheese, divided
1½ cups coarsely chopped ham
1½ cups (4 ounces) corkscrew pasta, cooked, drained
½ cup MIRACLE WHIP® or MIRACLE WHIP® LIGHT® Dressing
½ green or red bell pepper, chopped
¼ cup milk
Seasoned croutons (optional)

- Heat oven to 350°F.
- Mix all ingredients except ½ cup cheese and croutons.
- Spoon into 1½-quart casserole. Sprinkle with remaining ½ cup cheese.
- Bake 30 minutes or until thoroughly heated. Sprinkle with croutons, if desired.

Makes 4 to 6 servings

Cheesy Broccoli Bake

Citrus & Spice Pork Loin Roast

1 package (1.0 ounce) LAWRY'S® Taco Spices & Seasonings
¾ cup orange marmalade
½ teaspoon LAWRY'S® Garlic Powder with Parsley
1 boneless pork loin roast, about 3 to 3½ pounds

In small bowl, combine Taco Spices & Seasonings, orange marmalade and Garlic Powder with Parsley; mix well. Score pork roast with sharp knife. Place pork roast in large resealable plastic food storage bag and cover with marmalade mixture. Marinate in refrigerator 45 minutes. Remove pork from marinade; discard used marinade. Wrap pork in foil and place in baking dish. Bake in 350°F oven 1 hour. Open and fold back foil; bake 30 minutes longer or until roast is glazed and internal temperature reaches 170°F on a meat thermometer. Cool 10 minutes before slicing.

Makes 6 servings

Serving Suggestion: Slice pork thinly and serve drippings that remain in foil as a flavorful gravy. Garnish with parsley and orange peel, if desired.

Spam® and Rice Casserole

1 (12-ounce) can SPAM® Luncheon Meat, cubed
2 cups cooked white rice
½ cup chopped water chestnuts
½ cup sliced celery
¼ cup sliced green onions
¼ teaspoon black pepper
1 (10¾-ounce) can condensed cream of mushroom soup
⅓ cup mayonnaise or salad dressing

Heat oven to 350°F. In medium bowl, combine SPAM®, rice, water chestnuts, celery, green onions and pepper. In small bowl, combine soup and mayonnaise; mix with SPAM® mixture. Spoon into 1½-quart casserole. Bake 35 to 40 minutes or until thoroughly heated.

Makes 4 to 6 servings

Onion-Apple Glazed Pork Tenderloin

Prep Time: 5 minutes
Cook Time: 25 minutes

1 (1½- to 2-pound) boneless pork tenderloin
Ground black pepper
2 tablespoons olive or vegetable oil, divided
1 envelope LIPTON® RECIPE SECRETS® Onion Soup Mix
½ cup apple juice
2 tablespoons firmly packed brown sugar
¾ cup water
¼ cup dry red wine or water
1 tablespoon all-purpose flour

1. Preheat oven to 425°F. In small roasting pan or baking pan, arrange pork. Season with pepper and rub with 1 tablespoon oil. Roast uncovered 10 minutes.

2. Meanwhile, in small bowl, combine 1 tablespoon remaining oil, soup mix, apple juice and brown sugar. Pour over pork and continue roasting 10 minutes or until desired doneness. Remove pork to serving platter; cover with aluminum foil.

3. Place roasting pan over medium-high heat and bring pan juices to a boil, scraping up any browned bits from bottom of pan. Stir in water, wine and flour; boil, stirring constantly, 1 minute or until thickened.

4. To serve, thinly slice pork and serve with gravy.

Makes 4 to 6 servings

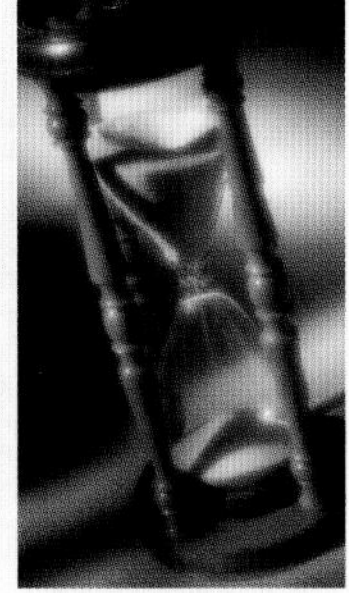

Quick Tip

Pork tenderloin is a very tender strip of pork that comes from the loin. Trim away and discard the fat from the tenderloin before cooking. Since the tenderloin is boneless, there is very little waste.

Biscuit-Topped Deep Dish Ham Bake

Filling

1 tablespoon Butter Flavor CRISCO® Stick or 1 tablespoon Butter Flavor CRISCO® all-vegetable shortening plus additional for greasing
1½ cups cut fresh green beans
2 medium carrots, cut into julienne strips
1 medium onion, chopped
½ cup thinly sliced celery
½ cup water
¼ cup all-purpose flour
1 tablespoon minced fresh parsley *or* 1 teaspoon dried parsley leaves
½ teaspoon Italian seasoning (dried thyme, oregano or basil can be substituted)
¼ teaspoon salt
¼ teaspoon black pepper
2 cups milk
1½ teaspoons instant chicken bouillon granules
2 cups cut-up cooked ham

Biscuits

1 cup all-purpose flour
1 tablespoon minced fresh parsley *or* 1 teaspoon dried parsley leaves
1½ teaspoons baking powder
¼ teaspoon salt
2 tablespoons Butter Flavor CRISCO® Stick or 2 tablespoons Butter Flavor CRISCO® all-vegetable shortening
½ cup milk

1. Heat oven to 375°F. Grease 2-quart casserole with shortening.

2. For filling, melt 1 tablespoon shortening in large saucepan. Add green beans, carrots, onion and celery. Cook and stir on medium heat until onion is tender. Add water. Heat to a boil. Reduce heat. Cover. Simmer about 12 minutes or until carrots are tender.

3. Stir in ¼ cup flour, 1 tablespoon parsley, Italian seasoning, ¼ teaspoon salt and pepper. Stir in 2 cups milk and bouillon granules. Cook and stir on medium heat until mixture thickens and comes to a boil. Remove from heat. Stir in ham. Pour into prepared casserole.

4. For biscuits, combine 1 cup flour, 1 tablespoon parsley, baking powder and ¼ teaspoon salt in small bowl. Cut in 2 tablespoons shortening using pastry blender (or 2 knives) until coarse crumbs form. Add ½ cup milk. Stir with fork until blended. Drop by spoonfuls on top of casserole to form 8 biscuits. Bake 35 to 40 minutes or until bubbly and biscuits are browned. *Do not overbake.* *Makes 4 to 6 servings*

Potato-Ham Scallop

2 cups cubed HILLSHIRE FARM® Ham
6 potatoes, peeled and thinly sliced
¼ cup chopped onion
⅓ cup all-purpose flour
Salt and black pepper to taste
2 cups milk
3 tablespoons bread crumbs
1 tablespoon butter or margarine, melted

Preheat oven to 350°F.

Place ½ of Ham in medium casserole. Cover with ½ of potatoes and ½ of onion. Sift ½ of flour over onions; sprinkle with salt and pepper. Repeat layers with remaining ham, potatoes, onion, flour, salt and pepper. Pour milk over casserole. Bake, covered, 1¼ hours. Combine bread crumbs and butter in small bowl; sprinkle over top of casserole. Bake, uncovered, 15 minutes or until topping is golden brown.

Makes 6 servings

Country Sausage Macaroni and Cheese

1 pound BOB EVANS® Special Seasonings Roll Sausage
1½ cups milk
12 ounces pasteurized processed Cheddar cheese, cut into cubes
½ cup Dijon mustard
1 cup diced fresh or drained canned tomatoes
1 cup sliced mushrooms
⅓ cup sliced green onions
⅛ teaspoon cayenne pepper
12 ounces uncooked elbow macaroni
2 tablespoons grated Parmesan cheese

Preheat oven to 350°F. Crumble and cook sausage in medium skillet until browned. Drain on paper towels. Combine milk, processed cheese and mustard in medium saucepan; cook and stir over low heat until cheese melts and mixture is smooth. Stir in sausage, tomatoes, mushrooms, green onions and cayenne pepper. Remove from heat.

Cook macaroni according to package directions; drain. Combine hot macaroni and cheese mixture in large bowl; toss until well coated. Spoon into greased 2-quart shallow casserole dish. Cover and bake 15 to 20 minutes. Stir; sprinkle with Parmesan cheese. Bake, uncovered, 5 minutes more. Let stand 10 minutes before serving. Refrigerate leftovers. *Makes 6 to 8 servings*

Country Sausage Macaroni and Cheese

Sausage and Broccoli Noodle Casserole

Prep Time: 15 minutes
Cook Time: 30 minutes

1 jar (16 ounces) RAGÚ® Cheese Creations!® Classic Alfredo Sauce
⅓ cup milk
1 pound sweet Italian sausage, cooked and crumbled
1 package (9 ounces) frozen chopped broccoli, thawed
8 ounces egg noodles, cooked and drained
1 cup shredded Cheddar cheese (about 4 ounces)
¼ cup chopped roasted red peppers

1. Preheat oven to 350°F. In large bowl, combine Ragú® Cheese Creations!® Sauce and milk. Stir in sausage, broccoli, noodles, ¾ cup cheese and roasted peppers.

2. In 13×9-inch baking dish, evenly spread sausage mixture. Sprinkle with remaining ¼ cup cheese.

3. Bake 30 minutes or until heated through. *Makes 6 servings*

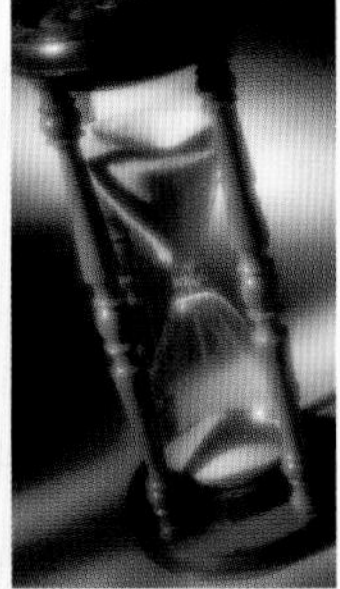

Quick Tip

Bulk sausage is the best choice for this recipe. If only link sausage is available, remove it from its casings by slitting the casing at one end of each link with the point of a sharp paring knife.

Sausage and Broccoli Noodle Casserole

Shrimp Alfredo with Sugar Snap Peas

Prep Time: 5 minutes
Cook Time: 15 minutes

½ cup milk
3 tablespoons margarine or butter
1 (4.7-ounce) package PASTA RONI® Fettuccine Alfredo
1 (9-ounce) package frozen sugar snap peas, thawed
8 ounces cooked, peeled, deveined medium shrimp
½ teaspoon ground lemon pepper

1. In large saucepan, bring 1¼ cups water, milk, margarine, pasta and Special Seasonings to a boil. Reduce heat to low. Gently boil 4 minutes, stirring occasionally.

2. Stir in snap peas, shrimp and lemon pepper; cook 1 to 2 minutes or until pasta is tender. Let stand 3 minutes before serving. *Makes 4 servings*

Tip: If you don't have lemon pepper in your cupboard, try Italian seasoning instead.

Shrimp Alfredo with Sugar Snap Peas

Crab Cakes with Tomato Salsa

Crab Cakes

1 pound crabmeat
1 tablespoon FILIPPO BERIO® Olive Oil
1 onion, finely chopped
1 cup fresh white bread crumbs, divided
2 eggs, beaten, divided
2 tablespoons drained capers, rinsed and chopped
2 tablespoons mayonnaise
1 tablespoon chopped fresh parsley
1 tablespoon ketchup
Finely grated peel of half a lemon
1 tablespoon lemon juice
Salt and freshly ground black pepper
Additional FILIPPO BERIO® Olive Oil for frying

Tomato Salsa

3 tablespoons FILIPPO BERIO® Olive Oil
4 large tomatoes, finely chopped
2 cloves garlic, crushed
¼ cup lemon juice
4½ teaspoons sweet or hot chili sauce
1 tablespoon sugar

For Crab Cakes, pick out and discard any shell or cartilage from crabmeat. Place crabmeat in medium bowl; flake finely. In small skillet, heat 1 tablespoon olive oil over medium heat until hot. Add onion; cook and stir 3 to 5 minutes or until softened. Add onion, ½ cup bread crumbs, 1 egg, capers, mayonnaise, parsley, ketchup, lemon peel and lemon juice to crabmeat; mix gently. Shape into 8 cakes; cover and refrigerate 30 minutes.

Meanwhile, for Tomato Salsa, in medium skillet, heat olive oil over medium heat until hot. Add tomatoes and garlic; cook and stir 5 minutes. Add lemon juice, chili sauce and sugar; mix well. Season to taste with salt and pepper.

Dip crab cakes into remaining beaten egg, then in remaining ½ cup bread crumbs. Press crumb coating firmly onto crab cakes.

In large nonstick skillet, pour in just enough olive oil to cover bottom. Heat over medium-high heat until hot. Add crab cakes; fry 5 to 8 minutes, turning frequently, until cooked through and golden brown. Drain on paper towels. Season to taste with salt and pepper. Serve hot with Tomato Salsa for dipping. *Makes 8 crab cakes*

Crab Cakes with Tomato Salsa

Grilled Jumbo Shrimp

24 raw jumbo shrimp, shelled and deveined
1 cup WESSON® Canola Oil
½ cup minced fresh onion
2 teaspoons dried oregano
1 teaspoon salt
1 teaspoon crushed fresh garlic
½ teaspoon dried basil
½ teaspoon dried thyme
3 tablespoons fresh lemon juice
6 long bamboo skewers, soaked in water for 20 minutes

Rinse shrimp and pat dry; set aside. In a large bowl, whisk together Wesson® Oil and *next* 6 ingredients, ending with thyme. Reserve ⅓ cup marinade; set aside. Toss shrimp in remaining marinade; cover and refrigerate 3 hours, tossing occasionally. Stir in lemon juice; let stand at room temperature for 30 minutes. Meanwhile, preheat grill or broiler. Drain shrimp; discard marinade. Thread 4 shrimp per skewer. Grill shrimp, 4 inches over hot coals, 3 minutes per side or until pink, basting with reserved ⅓ cup marinade.

Makes 6 servings

Shrimp Fettuccine

1½ cups prepared HIDDEN VALLEY® Original Ranch® Salad Dressing & Seasoning Mix
¼ cup sour cream
¼ cup grated Parmesan cheese
½ pound fettuccine, cooked and drained
½ pound cooked shrimp, shelled and deveined
½ cup cooked peas
Additional Parmesan cheese (optional)

In small bowl, combine salad dressing & seasoning mix, sour cream and ¼ cup cheese. In large bowl, toss fettuccine with dressing mixture, shrimp and peas. Divide equally among 4 plates. Sprinkle with additional Parmesan cheese, if desired.

Makes 4 servings

Grilled Jumbo Shrimp

Shrimp Primavera Pot Pie

Prep and Cook Time: 30 minutes

1 can (10¾ ounces) condensed cream of shrimp soup, undiluted
1 package (12 ounces) frozen peeled uncooked medium shrimp
2 packages (1 pound each) frozen mixed vegetables, such as green beans, potatoes, onions and red peppers, thawed and drained
1 teaspoon dried dill weed
¼ teaspoon salt
¼ teaspoon black pepper
1 can (11 ounces) refrigerated breadstick dough

1. Preheat oven to 400°F. Heat soup in medium ovenproof skillet over medium-high heat 1 minute. Add shrimp; cook and stir 3 minutes or until shrimp begin to thaw. Stir in vegetables, dill, salt and pepper; mix well. Reduce heat to medium-low; cook and stir 3 minutes.

2. Unwrap breadstick dough; separate into 8 strips. Twist strips, cutting to fit skillet. Arrange attractively over shrimp mixture in crisscross pattern. Press ends of dough lightly to edges of skillet to secure. Bake 18 minutes or until crust is golden brown and shrimp mixture is bubbly. *Makes 4 to 6 servings*

Sicilian Shrimp

¼ cup olive oil
2 pounds raw jumbo shrimp, shelled and deveined
¼ cup finely chopped green onion, including tops
2 teaspoons LAWRY'S® Garlic Salt
⅛ teaspoon LAWRY'S® Lemon Pepper
2 tablespoons lemon juice

In large skillet, heat oil. Add all ingredients and cook over medium-high heat until shrimp are pink and tender. *Makes 6 servings*

Serving Suggestion: Serve with mixed vegetable salad and rice pilaf.

Shrimp Primavera Pot Pie

Velvet Shrimp

3 tablespoons unsalted butter
½ cup finely chopped green onion tops
1 tablespoon plus 1 teaspoon Chef Paul Prudhomme's Seafood Magic®, divided
½ teaspoon minced garlic
1 pound medium to large shelled, deveined shrimp
2 cups heavy cream, divided
2 tablespoons Basic Seafood Stock (recipe follows) or water (optional)
1 cup (4 ounces) shredded Muenster cheese
Hot cooked pasta or rice (preferably converted)

Melt butter in 10-inch skillet over high heat. When butter is sizzling, stir in green onions and 1 tablespoon Seafood Magic®. Cook about 1½ minutes and add garlic and shrimp. Cook and stir about 2 minutes, then add 1 cup cream and remaining 1 teaspoon Seafood Magic®. Stir and scrape any browned bits off side and bottom of skillet. Cook about 1 minute and stir in remaining 1 cup cream. Cook 1 minute, or just until shrimp are plump and pink. Remove shrimp with slotted spoon; set aside. Still over high heat, whisk cream mixture often as it comes to a boil, then whisk constantly. Cook, whisking, 2 or 3 minutes, then add stock, if desired, and cheese. Cook 1 minute more or until cheese has melted. Return shrimp to skillet. Stir to coat shrimp with sauce. Serve over pasta or rice. *Makes 4 servings*

Basic Seafood Stock

10 to 12 cups shrimp, crawfish or crab shells *or* 1½ to 2 pounds fish carcasses (heads and gills removed)
2 quarts cold water or enough to cover ingredients

Place shells in stockpot or heavy saucepan and cover with cold water. Bring water to a boil over high heat. Reduce heat to low and simmer about 30 minutes. Strain, cool and refrigerate until ready to use. Freeze for longer storage. *Makes about 1 quart*

Baked Stuffed Lobster Tails

Preparation Time: 25 minutes
Cook Time: 15 minutes
Total Time: 40 minutes

½ cup lightly toasted fine fresh bread crumbs
1 small onion, finely diced
¼ cup FLEISCHMANN'S® Original Margarine
¼ cup loosely packed fresh tarragon leaves *or* 4 teaspoons dried tarragon
1½ teaspoons fresh lemon juice
Salt and pepper, to taste
4 frozen spiny lobster tails, defrosted
4 metal skewers

1. Blend bread crumbs, onion, margarine, tarragon, lemon juice and salt and pepper in food processor until well combined. Set aside.

2. Partially fill a large pot fitted with a steamer basket with water and heat to a boil. Place the lobster tails in the steamer; cover the pot and steam over high heat for 5 minutes. Transfer lobster with tongs to a colander to drain.

3. Cut the soft underside of the tails out. With skewer, pierce the end of each tail and run the skewer through the tail meat to the other end.

4. Spread one fourth of the stuffing over the meat of each lobster tail. Arrange the tails on a baking sheet.

5. Bake in preheated 500°F oven on middle rack for 8 to 10 minutes or until the stuffing is crisp and golden and the meat is cooked through. *Makes 4 servings*

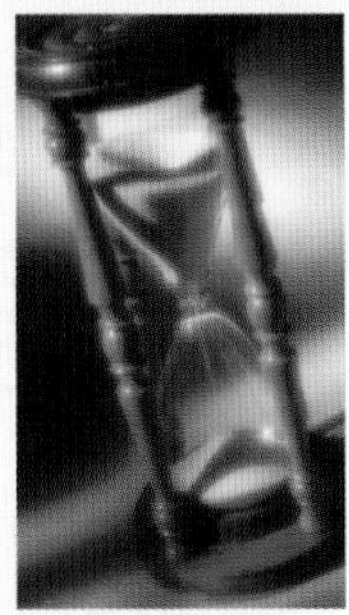

Quick Tip

To make fine fresh bread brumbs, tear lightly toasted bread slices into pieces and place in a food processor fitted with a metal blade. Process using on/off pulsing action until fine crumbs are formed.

Crustless Crab Florentine Quiche

1 can (6 ounces) crabmeat, well drained and flaked
½ package (10 ounces) frozen chopped spinach, thawed and well drained
½ cup chopped onion
1 cup fat-free shredded Cheddar cheese
4 SAUDER'S® large egg whites
2 SAUDER'S® large eggs
1 can (12 ounces) evaporated low-fat milk
½ teaspoon salt-free herb and spice blend

Line bottom of quiche dish or 9-inch pie plate with crabmeat. Top with spinach, onion and cheese. Blend egg whites, eggs, milk and seasoning. Pour over crabmeat mixture. Bake at 350°F for 45 minutes. Allow to stand 10 minutes before serving.

Makes 4 to 6 servings

Note: Canned crab is available as lump, claw meat or flaked. Once opened, keep canned crabmeat refrigerated and use within two days.

Crab Basil Fettuccine

3 tablespoons margarine or butter
3 tablespoons olive oil
2 tomatoes, peeled, seeded, chopped
1 garlic clove, minced
⅓ cup whipping cream
½ cup HOLLAND HOUSE® White Cooking Wine
½ cup chopped fresh basil
½ cup cooked fresh or frozen crabmeat
¼ cup freshly grated Parmesan cheese, divided
¼ cup chopped fresh parsley, divided
1 pound fettuccine, cooked, drained

Melt margarine and oil in medium saucepan over medium heat. Add tomatoes and garlic; simmer until tomatoes are softened. Add whipping cream and cooking wine; simmer 10 minutes. Stir in basil and crabmeat; simmer 3 minutes. Add ½ of cheese and ½ of parsley. Serve over cooked fettuccine. Sprinkle with remaining cheese and parsley.

Makes 6 servings

Crustless Crab Florentine Quiche

Mediterranean Shrimp & Vegetable Linguine

Prep Time: 15 minutes
Cook Time: 15 minutes

1 pound uncooked medium shrimp, peeled and deveined
3 teaspoons olive or vegetable oil
1 medium onion, finely chopped
1 large carrot, finely chopped
1 jar (26 to 28 ounces) RAGÚ® Light Pasta Sauce
1 box (16 ounces) linguine, cooked and drained

1. Season shrimp, if desired, with salt and ground black pepper. In 12-inch skillet, heat 2 teaspoons oil over medium-high heat and cook shrimp, stirring occasionally, 3 minutes or until almost pink. Remove shrimp and set aside.

2. In same skillet, heat remaining 1 teaspoon oil over medium-high heat and cook onion and carrot, stirring occasionally, 5 minutes or until vegetables are tender.

3. Stir in Ragú Pasta Sauce and bring to a boil over high heat. Reduce heat to low and simmer 5 minutes. Return shrimp to skillet and simmer until shrimp turn pink. Serve over hot linguine.

Makes 6 servings

Mediterranean Shrimp & Vegetable Linguine

Shrimp in Mock Lobster Sauce

½ cup reduced-sodium beef or chicken broth
¼ cup oyster sauce
1 tablespoon cornstarch
1 egg
1 egg white
1 tablespoon peanut or vegetable oil
¾ pound medium or large shrimp, peeled and deveined
2 cloves garlic, minced
3 green onions with tops, cut into ½-inch pieces
Hot cooked Chinese egg noodles

1. Stir broth and oyster sauce into cornstarch in small bowl until smooth. Beat egg with egg white in separate small bowl. Set aside.

2. Heat wok over medium-high heat 1 minute or until hot. Drizzle oil into wok and heat 30 seconds. Add shrimp and garlic; stir-fry 3 to 5 minutes or until shrimp turn pink and opaque.

3. Stir broth mixture; add to wok. Add onions; stir-fry 1 minute or until sauce boils and thickens.

4. Stir eggs into wok; stir-fry 1 minute or just until eggs are set. Serve over noodles.

Makes 4 servings

Note: Oyster sauce is a thick brown concentrated sauce made of ground oysters, soy sauce and brine. It imparts a slight fish flavor and is used as a seasoning. It is readily available in the Asian section of large supermarkets.

Shrimp in Mock Lobster Sauce

Shrimp & Ham Jambalaya

Preparation Time: 30 minutes
Cook Time: 20 minutes
Total Time: 50 minutes

1 onion, cut into wedges
1 large green bell pepper, chopped
2 cloves garlic, minced
¼ teaspoon ground red pepper
2 tablespoons FLEISCHMANN'S® Original Margarine
3 cups cooked rice
2 cups large shrimp, cleaned and cooked (about 1 pound)
2 cups cubed cooked ham (about 1¼ pounds)
1 (16-ounce) can peeled tomatoes, chopped (undrained)
1 teaspoon natural hickory seasoning

1. Cook and stir onion, bell pepper, garlic and red pepper in margarine in large skillet over medium heat until vegetables are tender.

2. Stir in remaining ingredients. Cook for 10 to 15 minutes or until heated through, stirring occasionally. Serve immediately.

Makes 8 servings

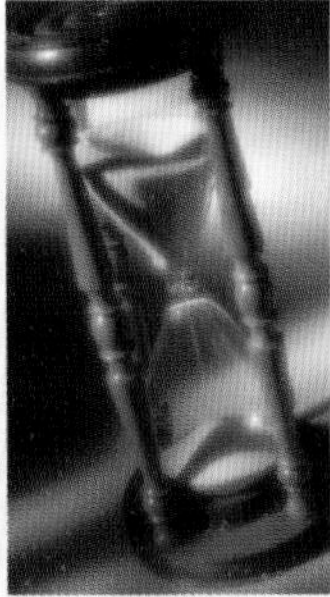

Quick Tip

To remove shells from shrimp, start at the large end and peel away the shell. To devein shrimp, cut a slit down the outside curve of the shrimp and under running water pull out the dark vein.

Shrimp & Ham Jambalaya

Creamy Salmon with Green Beans

1 large salmon fillet (about ¾ pound)
2 tablespoons butter or margarine
1 large ripe tomato, cut into ½-inch pieces
1 small onion, coarsely chopped
2 tablespoons all-purpose flour
1 cup vegetable or chicken broth
1 package (9 ounces) frozen cut green beans, partially thawed
1 cup half-and-half
¼ teaspoon salt
¼ teaspoon white pepper
5 tablespoons grated Parmesan cheese, divided
Hot cooked angel hair pasta

1. Rinse salmon and pat dry with paper towels. Remove skin and bones; discard. Cut salmon into ¾-inch pieces.

2. Heat wok over medium-high heat 1 minute or until hot. Add butter; swirl to coat bottom and heat 30 seconds. Add salmon; stir-fry gently 3 to 4 minutes or until fish flakes easily when tested with fork. Remove to large bowl; cover and keep warm.

3. Add tomato and onion to wok; stir-fry about 5 minutes or until onion is tender. Stir in flour until well mixed. Increase heat to high. Stir in broth and beans; cook until sauce boils and thickens. Add salmon, half-and-half, salt and pepper; cook until heated through. Add half of cheese; toss until well mixed. Spoon salmon mixture over angel hair pasta. Sprinkle with remaining cheese. Garnish, if desired.

Makes 4 servings

Creamy Salmon with Green Beans

Fish Françoise

Prep Time: 5 minutes
Cook Time: 19 minutes

1 can (14½ ounces) DEL MONTE® Diced Tomatoes with Garlic & Onion
1 tablespoon lemon juice
2 cloves garlic, minced
½ teaspoon dried tarragon leaves
⅛ teaspoon black pepper
3 tablespoons whipping cream
Vegetable oil
1½ pounds firm white fish fillets (such as halibut or cod)
Salt
Lemon wedges

1. Preheat broiler; position rack 4 inches from heat.

2. Combine undrained tomatoes, lemon juice, garlic, tarragon and pepper in large saucepan. Cook over medium-high heat about 10 minutes or until liquid has evaporated.

3. Stir in cream. Reduce heat to low. Cook until tomato mixture is very thick; set aside.

4. Brush broiler pan with oil. Arrange fish on pan; season with salt and additional pepper, if desired. Broil 3 to 4 minutes on each side or until fish flakes easily when tested with a fork.

5. Spread tomato mixture over top of fish. Broil 1 minute. Serve with lemon wedges.

Makes 4 servings

Fish Françoise

Creamy Tuna Broccoli and Swiss Sauce

Prep Time: 15 minutes

1 can (10¾ ounces) cream of broccoli soup
½ cup half-and-half
½ cup shredded Swiss cheese
2 cups chopped cooked broccoli*
1 jar (2 ounces) sliced pimiento, drained
1 (7-ounce) pouch of STARKIST® Premium Albacore or Chunk Light Tuna
Hot cooked pasta or rice

**Or substitute 1 package (10 ounces) frozen broccoli cuts, cooked and drained.*

In medium saucepan, combine soup, half-and-half and cheese; cook over low heat, stirring to blend well. Stir in broccoli, pimiento and tuna; continue cooking until sauce is thoroughly heated. Serve over pasta. *Makes 2 servings*

Fisherman's Style Linguine Fini

1 package (16 ounces) BARILLA® Linguine Fini
2 tablespoons extra-virgin olive oil
1 large leek, well rinsed and finely diced
½ teaspoon red pepper flakes
1 pound swordfish steak, skin removed, cut into ½-inch cubes
½ pound crab meat, shelled
½ cup heavy cream
¼ cup chopped fresh basil
½ teaspoon salt

1. Cook linguine according to package directions, reserving ½ cup cooking water before draining.

2. Meanwhile, heat olive oil in large skillet over medium heat. Add leek and red pepper flakes; cook and stir 5 minutes or until tender. Add swordfish, cook and stir 1 to 2 minutes or just until fish begins to turn opaque. Stir in crabmeat, heavy cream, basil and salt. Bring to a boil; cook 2 to 3 minutes or until sauce is slightly thickened.

3. Place hot drained linguine and reserved cooking water in serving bowl. Add swordfish and crab sauce; toss. Serve immediately. *Makes 6 servings*

Creamy Tuna Broccoli and Swiss Sauce

Flounder Stuffed with Crabmeat Imperial

2 whole baby flounder (about 1 to 1¼ pounds each)*
1 cup crabmeat, cleaned
¼ cup mayonnaise
2 tablespoons minced green bell pepper
1 teaspoon Worcestershire sauce
1 teaspoon prepared mustard
1 teaspoon chopped pimiento
Dash salt and black pepper
2 tablespoons seasoned bread crumbs
1 tablespoon melted butter

**Flat fish are generally sold as fillets. Whole flat fish, such as flounder, may need to be special ordered from your seafood retailer. Flounder should be gutted and scaled with head and tail left on.*

1. Preheat oven to 375°F.

2. Rinse flounder and pat dry with paper towels. Place fish on greased baking sheet with head side up. Cut slit down backbone of each fish, which is in the center of the top of the fish, using sharp utility knife.

3. Starting on 1 side of each fish, insert knife horizontally into slit. Begin cutting, about 1 inch from head, between flesh and bone, stopping just before tail to form pocket. Cut another pocket on other side of slit.

4. To make stuffing, pick out and discard any shell or cartilage from crabmeat. Combine crabmeat, mayonnaise, bell pepper, Worcestershire sauce, mustard, pimiento, salt and black pepper in small bowl. Spoon mixture evenly into prepared fish pockets.

5. Sprinkle fish with bread crumbs and drizzle with butter. Bake 25 minutes or until fish flakes easily when tested with fork. Garnish, if desired. *Makes 2 servings*

Flounder Stuffed with Crabmeat Imperial

Velveeta® Tuna & Noodles

Prep Time: 10 minutes
Cook Time: 15 minutes

2¼ cups water
3 cups (6 ounces) medium egg noodles, uncooked
¾ pound (12 ounces) VELVEETA® Pasteurized Prepared Cheese Product, cut up
1 package (16 ounces) frozen vegetable blend, thawed, drained
1 can (6 ounces) tuna, drained, flaked
¼ teaspoon black pepper

1. Bring water to boil in saucepan. Stir in noodles. Reduce heat to medium-low; cover. Simmer 8 minutes or until noodles are tender.

2. Add VELVEETA, vegetables, tuna and pepper; stir until VELVEETA is melted.

Makes 4 to 6 servings

Velveeta® Tuna & Noodles

Southern Fried Catfish with Hush Puppies

Hush Puppy Batter (recipe follows)
4 catfish fillets (about 1½ pounds)
½ cup yellow cornmeal
3 tablespoons all-purpose flour
1½ teaspoons salt
¼ teaspoon ground red pepper
Vegetable oil for frying
Fresh parsley sprigs for garnish

1. Prepare Hush Puppy Batter; set aside.

2. Rinse catfish and pat dry with paper towels. Combine cornmeal, flour, salt and red pepper in shallow dish. Dip fish in cornmeal mixture. Heat 1 inch of oil in large, heavy saucepan over medium heat until oil registers 375°F on deep-fry thermometer.

3. Fry fish, a few pieces at a time, 4 to 5 minutes or until golden brown and fish flakes easily when tested with fork. Adjust heat to maintain temperature. (Allow temperature of oil to return to 375°F between each batch.) Drain fish on paper towels.

4. To make Hush Puppies, drop batter by tablespoonfuls into hot oil. Fry, a few pieces at a time, 2 minutes or until golden brown. Garnish, if desired. *Makes 4 servings*

Hush Puppy Batter

1½ cups yellow cornmeal
½ cup all-purpose flour
2 teaspoons baking powder
½ teaspoon salt
1 cup milk
1 small onion, minced
1 egg, slightly beaten

Combine cornmeal, flour, baking powder and salt in medium bowl. Add milk, onion and egg. Stir until well combined. Allow batter to stand 5 to 10 minutes before frying. *Makes about 24 hush puppies*

Southern Fried Catfish with Hush Puppies

Mom's Tuna Casserole

2 cans (12 ounces each) tuna, drained and flaked
3 cups diced celery
3 cups crushed potato chips, divided
6 hard-cooked eggs, chopped
1 can (10¾ ounces) condensed cream of mushroom soup, undiluted
1 can (10¾ ounces) condensed cream of celery soup, undiluted
1 cup mayonnaise
1 teaspoon dried tarragon leaves
1 teaspoon black pepper

Slow Cooker Directions

Combine all ingredients, except ½ cup potato chips, in slow cooker; stir well. Top mixture with remaining ½ cup potato chips. Cover and cook on LOW 5 to 8 hours.

Makes 8 servings

Hazelnut-Coated Salmon Steaks

¼ cup hazelnuts
4 salmon steaks (about 5 ounces each)
1 tablespoon apple butter
1 tablespoon Dijon mustard
¼ teaspoon dried thyme leaves
⅛ teaspoon black pepper
2 cups hot cooked rice

1. Preheat oven to 375°F. Place hazelnuts on baking sheet; bake 8 minutes or until lightly browned. Quickly transfer nuts to clean dry dish towel. Fold towel; rub vigorously to remove as much of the skins as possible. Finely chop hazelnuts using food processor.

2. *Increase oven temperature to 450°F.* Place salmon in single layer in baking dish. Combine apple butter, mustard, thyme and pepper in small bowl. Brush on salmon; top each steak with nuts. Bake 14 to 16 minutes or until salmon flakes easily with fork. Serve with rice and steamed snow peas, if desired.

Makes 4 servings

Mom's Tuna Casserole

Spicy Fried Potatoes & Seasoned Fried Fish

Spicy Fried Potatoes
- **6 russet potatoes, washed and peeled**
- **⅔ cup bottled crawfish and seafood boil liquid concentrate**
- **½ cup warm water**
- **1½ tablespoons salt**
- **WESSON® Vegetable Oil**

Seasoned Fried Fish
- **2 pounds catfish fillets, cut into 1½- to 2-inch-wide strips**
- **Salt**
- **1½ (3-ounce) boxes seasoned fish fry dry mix**
- **WESSON® Vegetable Oil**

Spicy Fried Potatoes
Thinly slice potatoes smaller than French fries. Place slices in a bowl of water to prevent browning. In another small bowl, pour liquid concentrate, warm water and salt; stir until salt is dissolved. Drain water from potatoes; place potatoes in seasoned water and toss to coat. Cover and refrigerate potatoes for 2 hours, stirring occasionally. Drain in colander for 20 minutes before frying. Meanwhile, fill 2 deep-fry pots or electric skillets to half their depth with Wesson® Oil. Heat oil to 350°F.

Seasoned Fried Fish
Rinse fish and pat dry; sprinkle with salt. Dredge fish on both sides with seasoned fry mix; coat well.

Frying
In one deep-fry pot, fry fish, a few pieces at a time, until golden brown and crisp (about 2 to 3 minutes). In other deep-fry pot, fry potatoes, in small batches, until golden brown and crisp. Remove fish and potatoes from oil and drain on paper towels. Salt to taste; serve hot.

Makes 8 to 10 servings

Tip: For family members who don't like fish, substitute chicken tenders for the catfish.

Speedy Salmon Patties

1 can (12 ounces) pink salmon, undrained
¼ cup minced green onions
1 egg, lightly beaten
1 tablespoon chopped fresh dill
1 clove garlic, minced
½ cup all-purpose flour
1½ teaspoons baking powder
1½ cups vegetable oil

1. Drain salmon well; reserve 2 tablespoons liquid. Place salmon in medium bowl; break apart with fork. Add reserved liquid, green onions, egg, dill and garlic; mix well.

2. Combine flour and baking powder in small bowl; stir in salmon mixture until well blended. Divide mixture into 6 balls; shape into patties.

3. Heat oil in large skillet to 350°F. Add salmon patties; cook until golden brown on both sides. Remove from oil; drain on paper towels. Serve warm. *Makes 6 patties*

Tuna Skillet Supper

1 package (8 ounces) cream cheese, softened
1 cup milk
1 packet (1 ounce) HIDDEN VALLEY® Original Ranch® Salad Dressing & Seasoning Mix
8 ounces uncooked spiral egg noodles
2 cups frozen petite peas, thawed
2 cans (6 ounces each) tuna or shrimp, drained

In a food processor fitted with a metal blade, blend cream cheese, milk and salad dressing & seasoning mix until smooth.

Cook pasta according to package directions; drain and combine with peas and tuna in a large skillet. Stir dressing mixture into pasta. Cook over low heat until mixture is hot. *Makes 4 to 6 servings*

Southwestern Roasted Salmon & Corn

- 2 ears fresh corn, unhusked
- 1 (6-ounce) salmon fillet, cut into 2 equal pieces
- 1 tablespoon plus 1 teaspoon fresh lime juice, divided
- 1 clove garlic, minced
- ½ teaspoon chili powder
- ¼ teaspoon ground cumin
- ¼ teaspoon dried oregano leaves
- ⅛ teaspoon salt, divided
- ⅛ teaspoon black pepper
- 2 teaspoons margarine, melted
- 2 teaspoons minced fresh cilantro

1. Preheat oven to 400°F. Spray shallow 1-quart baking dish with nonstick cooking spray. Pull back husks from each ear of corn, leaving husks attached. Discard silk. Soak corn in cold water 20 minutes.

2. Place salmon, skin side down, in prepared dish. Pour 1 tablespoon lime juice over fillets. Marinate at room temperature 15 minutes.

3. Combine garlic, chili powder, cumin, oregano, half of salt and the pepper in small bowl. Pat salmon lightly with paper towel. Rub garlic mixture on tops and sides of salmon.

4. Remove corn from water; pat kernels dry with paper towels. Bring husks back up over each ear; secure at top with thin strips of corn husk. Place corn on one side of oven rack. Roast 10 minutes; turn.

5. Place salmon in baking dish on other side of oven rack. Roast 15 minutes or until salmon is opaque and flakes when tested with fork, and corn is tender.

6. Combine margarine, cilantro and remaining salt in small bowl. Remove husks from corn. Brush over corn. Serve corn with salmon. *Makes 2 servings*

Tip: Roasting corn gives it a special flavor. However, it may also be cooked in boiling water. Husk the corn. Omit step 4. Place in a large pot of boiling water. Cover; remove from heat and let stand for 10 minutes. Drain and brush with cilantro butter as directed.

Southwestern Roasted Salmon & Corn

Tempting Tuna Parmesano

Prep and Cook Time: 16 minutes

2 large cloves garlic
1 package (9 ounces) refrigerated fresh angel hair pasta
¼ cup butter or margarine
1 cup whipping cream
1 cup frozen peas
¼ teaspoon salt
1 can (6 ounces) white tuna in water, drained
¼ cup grated Parmesan cheese, plus additional cheese for serving
Black pepper

1. Fill large deep skillet ¾ full with water. Cover and bring to a boil over high heat. Meanwhile, peel and mince garlic.

2. Add pasta to skillet; boil 1 to 2 minutes or until pasta is al dente. *Do not overcook.* Drain; set aside.

3. Add butter and garlic to skillet; cook over medium-high heat until butter is melted and sizzling. Stir in cream, peas and salt; bring to a boil.

4. Break tuna into chunks and stir into skillet with ¼ cup cheese. Return pasta to skillet. Cook until heated through; toss gently. Serve with additional cheese and pepper to taste.

Makes 2 to 3 servings

Serving Suggestion: Serve with a tossed romaine and tomato salad with Italian dressing.

Tempting Tuna Parmesano

Grilled Fish Florentine

Marinade

¼ cup vegetable oil
2 tablespoons lemon juice
2 tablespoons soy sauce
1 teaspoon grated lemon peel
1 garlic clove, minced
4 fresh or frozen red snapper or swordfish fillets or steaks, thawed

Florentine Sauce

1 tablespoon butter
½ cup chopped scallions
¼ cup chopped fresh mushrooms
1 cup chicken broth
⅓ cup HOLLAND HOUSE® White Cooking Wine
½ cup whipping cream
4 cups chopped fresh spinach
¼ teaspoon pepper

1. For marinade, in large non-metallic bowl, combine oil, lemon juice, soy sauce, lemon peel and garlic; mix well. Add fish, turning to coat all sides. Cover; refrigerate 2 hours. Prepare barbecue grill.

2. Meanwhile, for florentine sauce, melt butter in large skillet over medium heat. Add scallons and mushrooms; cook until softened, about 3 minutes, stirring occasionally. Stir in chicken broth and cooking wine. Bring to a boil; boil until sauce is reduced by half, about 10 minutes. Add whipping cream; simmer over medium heat until sauce is reduced to about ½ cup, about 10 minutes. Strain into food processor bowl. Add spinach; process until smooth. Add pepper, keep warm.

3. Drain fish, reserving marinade. Place fish on grill over medium-hot coals. Cook 10 minutes or until fish flakes easily with a fork, turning once and brushing frequently with marinade.* Discard any leftover marinade. Serve fish with spinach sauce.

Makes 4 servings

**Do not brush with marinade during last 5 minutes of cooking.*

Grilled Fish Florentine

Baked Cut Ziti

- **1 package (16 ounces) BARILLA® Cut Ziti**
- **3 tablespoons butter**
- **3 tablespoons all-purpose flour**
- **½ teaspoon salt**
- **½ teaspoon pepper**
- **½ teaspoon dried oregano**
- **1½ cups milk**
- **4 ripe tomatoes (about 2 pounds), divided**
- **¼ cup Italian-flavored bread crumbs**
- **1 tablespoon olive oil**
- **½ cup grated Parmesan cheese**
- **¼ cup fresh basil leaves, chopped**

1. Cook ziti according to package directions; drain and set aside.

2. To prepare white sauce, melt butter in small saucepan over medium heat. Add flour, salt, pepper and oregano; cook and stir 1 minute or until bubbly. Gradually stir in milk; cook 2 to 3 minutes or until thickened, stirring constantly. Remove from heat.

3. Preheat oven to 350°F. Peel, seed and chop 3 tomatoes. Slice remaining tomato. Combine bread crumbs and olive oil in small cup.

4. Combine cooked ziti, white sauce, chopped tomatoes, cheese and basil in large bowl. Transfer to 2-quart baking dish; arrange tomato slices on top and sprinkle with bread crumbs. Bake 30 minutes. Cool slightly before serving.

Makes 6 to 8 servings

Baked Cut Ziti

Paris Pasta

Prep Time: 10 minutes
Cook Time: 15 minutes

2 tablespoons margarine or butter
2 cloves garlic, minced
½ cup milk
2 cups 1-inch asparagus pieces or very thin green beans
¼ teaspoon ground black pepper
1 (4.7-ounce) package PASTA RONI® Parmesano
½ cup diced roasted red bell peppers
½ cup chopped muenster cheese
¼ cup chopped fresh basil or parsley

1. In large saucepan over medium-high heat, melt margarine. Add garlic; sauté 1 minute.

2. Stir in 1⅓ cups water, milk, asparagus and black pepper. Bring to a boil.

3. Stir in pasta and Special Seasonings. Reduce heat to low. Gently boil uncovered, 5 to 6 minutes or until pasta is tender, stirring occasionally.

4. Stir in bell peppers and cheese. Remove from heat. Let stand 3 minutes or until cheese is melted. Top with basil.

Makes 4 servings

Paris Pasta

Beer and Cheese Soup

Prep and Cook Time: 20 minutes

2 to 3 slices pumpernickel or rye bread
3 tablespoons water
3 tablespoons cornstarch
¼ cup finely chopped onion
1 tablespoon butter or margarine
¾ teaspoon dried thyme leaves
2 cloves garlic, minced
1 can (about 14 ounces) chicken or vegetable broth
1 cup beer
1 cup (6 ounces) shredded or diced American cheese
1 to 1½ cups (4 to 6 ounces) shredded sharp Cheddar cheese
½ teaspoon paprika
1 cup milk

1. Preheat oven to 425°F. To prepare croutons, slice bread into ½-inch cubes; place on baking sheet. Bake 10 to 12 minutes, stirring once, or until crisp; set aside.

2. While bread is in oven, stir water into cornstarch in small bowl; set aside. Place onion, butter, thyme and garlic in 3-quart saucepan; cook over medium-high heat 3 to 4 minutes or until onion is tender. Add broth; bring to a boil. Stir in beer, cheeses and paprika. Reduce heat to low; whisk in milk and cornstarch mixture. Stir until cheese melts and soup bubbles and thickens. Ladle into bowls. Top with prepared croutons.

Makes 6 (1-cup) servings

Beer and Cheese Soup

Jamaican Black Bean Stew

2 cups uncooked brown rice
3 pounds butternut squash, peeled, seeded and cut into ¾-inch cubes (about 5 cups)
2 pounds sweet potatoes, peeled and cut into ¾-inch cubes (about 4 cups)
1 large onion, coarsely chopped
1 can (about 14 ounces) vegetable broth
3 cloves garlic, minced
1 tablespoon curry powder
1½ teaspoons ground allspice
½ teaspoon ground red pepper
¼ teaspoon salt
2 cans (15 ounces each) black beans, drained and rinsed
½ cup raisins
3 tablespoons fresh lime juice
1 cup diced tomato
1 cup diced, peeled cucumber

1. Prepare rice according to package directions.

2. Combine squash, potatoes, onion, broth, garlic, curry powder, allspice, pepper and salt in Dutch oven. Bring to a boil; reduce heat to low. Simmer, covered, 5 minutes. Add beans and raisins. Simmer 5 minutes or just until sweet potatoes and squash are tender and beans are hot. Remove from heat; stir in lime juice.

3. Serve stew over brown rice and top with tomato and cucumber.

Makes 8 servings

Jamaican Black Bean Stew

Velveeta® Ultimate Macaroni & Cheese

Prep Time: 5 minutes
Cook Time: 15 minutes

2 cups (8 ounces) elbow macaroni, uncooked
1 pound (16 ounces) VELVEETA® Pasteurized Prepared Cheese Product, cut up
½ cup milk
Dash pepper

1. Cook macaroni as directed on package; drain well. Return to same pan.

2. Add VELVEETA, milk and pepper to same pan. Stir on low heat until VELVEETA is melted. Serve immediately. *Makes 4 to 6 servings*

Green Enchiladas with Spicy Sauce

½ cup salad oil
1 dozen corn tortillas
2 cups (8 ounces) shredded Monterey Jack cheese
¾ cup chopped green onions
2 packages (1.0 ounce each) LAWRY'S® Gravy Mix for Chicken
2 cups water
1 cup dairy sour cream
1 can (4 ounces) diced green chiles
Chunky salsa

Preheat oven to 425°F. In medium skillet, heat oil. Cook tortillas, one at a time, in hot oil for 15 seconds on each side. (Do not overcook or they won't roll.) In medium bowl, combine cheese and onions. Place 3 tablespoons on each tortilla; roll up. Place seam side down in 12×8×2-inch baking dish. In medium saucepan, prepare both Gravy Mix packages for Chicken with water according to package directions. Stir in sour cream and chiles; heat thoroughly but do not boil. Pour over tortillas. Bake at 425°F. in oven for 20 minutes. Sprinkle remaining cheese mixture on top; return to oven 5 minutes longer or until cheese melts. *Makes 6 servings*

Serving Suggestion: Serve salsa over top.

Velveeta® Ultimate Macaroni & Cheese

Spicy Tomato, Onion and Cheese Tart

Prep Time: 20 minutes
Cook Time: 40 minutes

- **1 package (11 ounces) pie crust mix**
- **⅓ cup cold water**
- **2 tablespoons olive oil**
- **3 cups thinly sliced red onions**
- **3 tablespoons *Frank's® RedHot®* Cayenne Pepper Sauce**
- **¾ teaspoon dried tarragon leaves**
- **1½ cups (6 ounces) shredded Monterey Jack cheese, divided**
- **4 ripe plum tomatoes, thinly sliced, divided**

1. Preheat oven to 450°F. Prepare pie crust mix according to package directions using water. Roll out dough to 14-inch circle on lightly floured board. Press dough into 12-inch pizza pan, folding edges under to fit inside pan. Prick dough with fork. Bake 15 minutes or until bottom of crust is golden brown. (Cover pan loosely with foil if crust browns too quickly.) Cool. Remove from oven. *Reduce oven temperature to 375°F.*

2. Heat oil in large nonstick skillet over medium heat. Add onions; cook and stir 5 minutes or until softened. Stir in ***Frank's RedHot*** Sauce and tarragon. Cook, covered, 5 minutes or until onions are very tender, stirring occasionally.

3. Sprinkle ¾ cup cheese over crust. Top with half of the tomatoes and cover with onions. Layer remaining ¾ cup cheese and tomatoes over onions. Bake 15 minutes or until cheese melts and tomatoes soften. Let stand 10 minutes. Cut into thin wedges to serve.

Makes 12 servings

Three Cheese Vegetable Lasagna

1 teaspoon olive oil
1 large onion, chopped
3 cloves garlic, minced
1 can (28 ounces) no-salt-added tomato purée
1 can (14½ ounces) no-salt-added tomatoes, undrained and chopped
2 cups (6 ounces) sliced fresh mushrooms
1 medium zucchini, finely chopped
1 large green bell pepper, chopped
2 teaspoons dried basil leaves, crushed
1 teaspoon salt (optional)
1 teaspoon sugar (optional)
½ teaspoon red pepper flakes
½ teaspoon dried oregano leaves, crushed
2 cups (15 ounces) SARGENTO® Light Ricotta Cheese
1 package (10 ounces) frozen chopped spinach, thawed and squeezed dry
2 egg whites
2 tablespoons (½ ounce) SARGENTO® Fancy Parmesan Shredded Cheese
8 ounces lasagna noodles, cooked according to package directions, without oil or salt
¾ cup (3 ounces) SARGENTO® Light Mozzarella Cheese, divided
¾ cup (3 ounces) SARGENTO® Mild Cheddar Shredded Cheese, divided

Spray large skillet with nonstick vegetable spray. Add oil and heat over medium heat; add onion and garlic. Cook until tender, stirring occasionally. Add tomato purée, tomatoes and liquid, mushrooms, zucchini, bell pepper, basil, salt, sugar, pepper flakes and oregano. Bring to a boil; reduce heat to low. Cover and simmer 10 minutes or until vegetables are crisp-tender.

Combine Ricotta cheese, spinach, egg whites and Parmesan cheese in medium bowl; mix well. Spread 1 cup sauce in bottom of 13×9-inch baking dish. Layer 3 lasagna noodles over sauce. Top with half the Ricotta cheese mixture and 2 cups remaining sauce. Repeat layering with 3 more lasagna noodles, remaining Ricotta mixture and 2 cups sauce. Combine Mozzarella and Cheddar cheeses. Sprinkle ¾ cup cheese mixture over sauce. Top with remaining lasagna noodles and sauce. Cover with foil; bake at 375°F 30 minutes. Uncover; bake 15 minutes more. Sprinkle with remaining ¾ cup cheese mixture. Let stand 10 minutes before serving. *Makes 10 servings*

Layered Mexican Tortilla Cheese Casserole

1 can (14½ ounces) salsa-style or Mexican-style stewed tomatoes, undrained
½ cup chopped fresh cilantro, divided
2 tablespoons fresh lime juice
Nonstick vegetable cooking spray
6 (6-inch) corn tortillas, torn into 1½-inch pieces
1 can (15 ounces) black beans, rinsed and drained
1 can (8 ounces) whole kernel corn, drained *or* 1 cup frozen whole kernel corn, thawed
2 cups (8 ounces) SARGENTO® Mexican Blend Shredded Cheese

1. In small bowl, combine tomatoes, ¼ cup cilantro and lime juice; set aside.

2. Coat 8-inch square baking dish with cooking spray. Arrange ¼ of tortillas in bottom of dish; spoon ¼ of tomato mixture over tortillas. Top with ¼ of beans, ¼ of corn and ¼ of cheese. Repeat layering 3 more times with remaining tortillas, tomato mixture, beans, corn and cheese.

3. Bake uncovered at 375°F for 25 minutes or until cheese is melted and sauce is bubbly. Sprinkle with remaining ¼ cup cilantro. Let stand 10 minutes before serving.

Makes 4 servings

Cappelini with Creamed Spinach and Feta Cheese

1 package (16 ounces) BARILLA® Cappelini
2 packages (9 ounces each) frozen creamed spinach
2 packages (4 ounces each) crumbled feta cheese

1. Cook cappelini according to package directions; drain.

2. Meanwhile, microwave spinach according to package directions. Combine hot spinach and cheese in large serving bowl.

3. Add hot drained cappelini to spinach mixture; toss.

Makes 8 servings

Layered Mexican Tortilla Cheese Casserole

Three Cheese Baked Ziti

1 container (15 ounces) part-skim ricotta cheese
2 eggs, beaten
¼ cup grated Parmesan cheese
1 box (16 ounces) ziti pasta, cooked and drained
1 jar (28 ounces) RAGÚ® Chunky Gardenstyle Pasta Sauce
1 cup shredded mozzarella cheese (about 4 ounces)

Preheat oven to 350°F. In large bowl, combine ricotta cheese, eggs and Parmesan cheese; set aside.

In another bowl, thoroughly combine pasta and Ragú® Chunky Gardenstyle Pasta Sauce.

In 13×9-inch baking dish, spoon ½ of the pasta mixture; evenly top with ricotta cheese mixture, then remaining pasta mixture. Sprinkle with mozzarella cheese. Bake 30 minutes or until heated through. Serve, if desired, with additional heated pasta sauce.

Makes 8 servings

Hearty Lentil Stew

2 tablespoons BERTOLLI® Olive Oil
3 medium carrots, sliced
3 ribs celery, sliced
1 cup lentils
3 cups water, divided
1 envelope LIPTON® RECIPE SECRETS® Savory Herb with Garlic Soup Mix*
1 tablespoon cider vinegar or red wine vinegar
Hot cooked brown rice, couscous or pasta

**Also terrific with LIPTON® RECIPE SECRETS® Onion-Mushroom or Onion Soup Mix.*

In 3-quart saucepan, heat oil over medium heat and cook carrots and celery, stirring occasionally, 3 minutes. Add lentils and cook 1 minute. Stir in 2 cups water. Bring to a boil over high heat. Reduce heat to low and simmer covered, stirring occasionally, 25 minutes. Stir in soup mix blended with remaining 1 cup water. Simmer covered additional 10 minutes or until lentils are tender. Stir in vinegar. Serve over hot rice.

Makes about 4 servings

Three Cheese Baked Ziti

Classic Fettuccine Alfredo

- ¾ pound uncooked fettuccine
- 6 tablespoons unsalted butter
- ⅔ cup heavy or whipping cream
- ½ teaspoon salt
- Generous dash white pepper
- Generous dash ground nutmeg
- 1 cup freshly grated Parmesan cheese (about 3 ounces)
- 2 tablespoons chopped fresh Italian parsley
- Fresh Italian parsley sprig for garnish

1. Cook fettuccine in large pot of boiling salted water 6 to 8 minutes until tender but slightly firm. Drain well; return to dry pot.

2. Place butter and cream in large, heavy skillet over medium-low heat. Cook and stir until butter melts and mixture bubbles. Cook and stir 2 minutes more. Stir in salt, pepper and nutmeg. Remove from heat. Gradually stir in cheese until thoroughly blended and smooth. Return briefly to heat to completely blend cheese if necessary. (Do not let sauce bubble or cheese will become lumpy and tough.)

3. Pour sauce over fettuccine in pot. Stir and toss with 2 forks over low heat for 2 to 3 minutes until sauce is thickened and fettuccine is evenly coated. Sprinkle with chopped parsley. Garnish, if desired. Serve immediately. *Makes 4 servings*

Baked Manicotti

- 1 jar (26 ounces) RAGÚ® Old World Style® Pasta Sauce
- 8 fresh or frozen prepared manicotti
- ½ cup shredded mozzarella cheese (about 2 ounces)
- 2 tablespoons grated Parmesan cheese

Preheat oven to 450°F. In 13×9-inch baking dish, spread ½ of the Ragú® Pasta Sauce; arrange manicotti over sauce. Top with remaining sauce. Sprinkle with cheeses. Bake covered 20 minutes. Remove cover and continue baking 5 minutes or until heated through. *Makes 4 servings*

Classic Fettuccine Alfredo

Cheesy Deluxe Primavera Mac Skillet

Prep Time: 5 minutes
Cook Time: 15 minutes

2⅓ cups water
1 package (14 ounces) KRAFT® Light Deluxe Macaroni & Cheese Dinner
½ teaspoon dried basil leaves, crushed
½ teaspoon garlic powder
3 cups frozen vegetable medley (broccoli, cauliflower and carrots)

BRING water to boil in large skillet. Stir in Macaroni and seasonings; return to a boil.

STIR in vegetables. Reduce heat to medium-low; cover. Simmer 10 minutes or until macaroni is tender.

STIR in Cheese Sauce. Cook and stir 2 minutes on medium-high heat until thickened and creamy.

Makes 5 servings

Cheesy Deluxe Primavera Mac Skillet

Potato Soup with Green Chilies & Cheese

2 tablespoons vegetable oil
1 medium onion, chopped
1 clove garlic, minced
2 cups chopped unpeeled potatoes
1 tablespoon all-purpose flour
1½ cups chicken or vegetable broth
2 cups milk
1 can (4 ounces) diced green chilies, undrained
½ teaspoon celery salt
¾ cup (3 ounces) shredded Monterey Jack cheese
¾ cup (3 ounces) shredded Colby or Cheddar cheese
White pepper
Chopped celery leaves for garnish

Heat oil in 3-quart pan over medium heat. Add onion and garlic; cook until onion is tender. Stir in potatoes; cook 1 minute. Stir in flour; continue cooking 1 minute. Stir in broth. Bring to a boil. Cover; reduce heat and simmer 20 minutes or until potatoes are tender. Stir in milk, chilies and celery salt; heat to simmering. Add cheeses; stir and heat just until cheeses melt. *Do not boil.* Add pepper to taste. Serve in individual bowls. Garnish with celery leaves. *Makes 6 servings*

Easy Fettuccine Alfredo

Prep: 15 minutes
Cook: 10 minutes

1 package (8 ounces) PHILADELPHIA® Cream Cheese, cubed
1 cup KRAFT® Shredded Parmesan Cheese
½ cup (1 stick) butter or margarine
½ cup milk
8 ounces fettuccine, cooked, drained

MIX cream cheese, Parmesan cheese, butter and milk in large saucepan; cook on low heat until cream cheese is completely melted, stirring occasionally.

ADD fettuccine; toss lightly. Serve with additional Parmesan cheese, if desired.
Makes 4 servings

Potato Soup with Green Chilies & Cheese

Double Cheese Strata

Prep Time: 15 minutes
Cook Time: 35 minutes
Stand Time: 10 minutes

10 to 12 slices Italian bread, about ½ inch thick
⅔ cup (about 5 ounces) sharp Cheddar light cold pack cheese food, softened
1⅓ cups *French's*® French Fried Onions
1 package (10 ounces) frozen chopped broccoli, thawed and drained
½ cup (2 ounces) shredded Swiss cheese
5 eggs
3 cups milk
2 tablespoons *French's*® Zesty Deli Mustard
½ teaspoon salt
¼ teaspoon ground white pepper

Grease shallow 3-quart baking dish. Spread bread slices with Cheddar cheese. Arrange slices in a single layer in bottom of prepared baking dish, pressing to fit. Layer French Fried Onions, broccoli and Swiss cheese over bread.

Beat together eggs, milk, mustard, salt and pepper in medium bowl until well blended. Pour egg mixture over layers. Let stand 10 minutes. Preheat oven to 350°F. Bake 35 minutes or until knife inserted in center comes out clean. (Cover loosely with foil near end of baking if top becomes too brown.) Cool on wire rack 10 minutes. Cut into squares to serve.

Makes 8 servings

Creamy Shells with Spinach and Mushrooms

1 package (16 ounces) BARILLA® Medium or Large Shells
1 can (12 ounces) evaporated milk
1 cup (4 ounces) grated Parmesan cheese, divided
4 ounces brick cheese, cubed (about ¾ cup)
4 tablespoons butter or margarine
2 tablespoons olive or vegetable oil
1 small onion, chopped
3 cloves garlic, minced
2 packages (10 ounces each) frozen chopped spinach, thawed and well drained
1½ cups (4 ounces) sliced mushrooms

1. Cook pasta shells according to package directions; drain.

2. Meanwhile, heat evaporated milk, Parmesan (reserving 2 tablespoons for topping) and brick cheese in small saucepan over medium heat until cheeses melt, stirring frequently. Set aside.

3. Heat butter and oil in large skillet over medium-high heat. Add onion and garlic; cook about 5 minutes, stirring occasionally, until onion is transparent. Add spinach and mushrooms; cook 5 minutes, stirring occasionally.

4. Stir cheese mixture into skillet; mix well. Pour over hot drained pasta shells on platter; sprinkle with reserved Parmesan. *Makes 8 servings*

Risotto alla Milanese

¼ teaspoon saffron threads
3½ to 4 cups chicken or vegetable broth
7 tablespoons butter or margarine, divided
1 large onion, chopped
1½ cups uncooked arborio or short-grain white rice
½ cup dry white wine
½ teaspoon salt
Dash pepper
¼ cup freshly grated Parmesan cheese
Chopped fresh parsley, fresh parsley sprig and tomato slices for garnish

1. Crush saffron in mortar with pestle to a powder. Place saffron in glass measuring cup.

2. Bring broth to a boil in small saucepan over medium heat; reduce heat to low. Stir ½ cup broth into saffron to dissolve; set aside. Keep remaining broth hot.

3. Heat 6 tablespoons butter in large, heavy skillet or 2½-quart saucepan over medium heat until melted and bubbly. Cook and stir onion in hot butter 5 minutes or until onion is soft. Stir in rice; cook and stir 2 minutes. Stir in wine, salt and pepper. Cook, uncovered, over medium-high heat 3 to 5 minutes until wine has evaporated, stirring occasionally.

4. Measure ½ cup hot broth; stir into rice mixture. Reduce heat to medium-low, maintaining a simmer throughout steps 4 and 5. Cook and stir until broth has absorbed. Repeat, adding ½ cup broth 3 more times, cooking and stirring after each addition until broth has absorbed.

5. Add saffron-flavored broth to rice and cook until absorbed. Continue adding remaining broth, ½ cup at a time, cooking and stirring until rice is tender but firm and mixture has slightly creamy consistency. (Not all the broth may be necessary. Total cooking time of rice will be about 20 minutes.)

6. Remove risotto from heat. Stir in remaining 1 tablespoon butter and cheese. Garnish, if desired. Serve immediately. *Makes 6 to 8 servings*

Risotto alla Milanese

Salsa Macaroni & Cheese

Prep Time: 5 minutes
Cook Time: 15 minutes

1 jar (16 ounces) RAGÚ® Cheese Creations!® Double Cheddar Sauce
1 cup prepared mild salsa
8 ounces elbow macaroni, cooked and drained

1. In 2-quart saucepan, heat Ragú Cheese Creations! Sauce over medium heat. Stir in salsa; heat through.

2. Toss with hot macaroni. Serve immediately. *Makes 4 servings*

Wisconsin Asiago Corn Risotto

2 cans (15 ounces each) vegetable broth
1 cup (8 ounces) carrot juice
2 tablespoons olive oil
1 onion, coarsely chopped
1 tablespoon coarsely chopped garlic
1 cup uncooked arborio or short-grain rice
1 bag (16 ounces) frozen corn, thawed and drained
¼ cup chopped fresh Italian parsley
2 teaspoons chopped fresh thyme or rosemary *or* 1 teaspoon dried herbs
½ cup (2 ounces) grated Wisconsin Parmesan cheese
½ cup (2 ounces) grated Wisconsin Romano cheese
½ teaspoon pepper
1 teaspoon chopped chives
1 cup (4 ounces) Wisconsin Asiago cheese shavings

In 2-quart saucepan heat broth and carrot juice until simmering. In Dutch oven, heat olive oil until sizzling; add onion, garlic and rice. Cook over medium heat; adding 1 cup simmering broth mixture. Stir rice constantly; gradually add remaining broth mixture, allowing liquid to be absorbed before adding more, 25 to 30 minutes. Add corn, parsley and thyme; stir in Parmesan and Romano. Sprinkle with pepper and chives; top with shavings of Asiago. *Makes 6 servings*

Favorite recipe from *Wisconsin Milk Marketing Board*

Salsa Macaroni & Cheese

Hearty Vegetable Gumbo

Nonstick cooking spray
½ cup chopped onion
½ cup chopped green bell pepper
¼ cup chopped celery
2 cloves garlic, minced
2 cans (about 14 ounces each) no-salt-added stewed tomatoes, undrained
2 cups no-salt-added tomato juice
1 can (15 ounces) red beans, rinsed and drained
1 tablespoon chopped fresh parsley
¼ teaspoon dried oregano leaves
¼ teaspoon hot pepper sauce
2 bay leaves
1½ cups uncooked, quick-cooking brown rice
1 package (10 ounces) frozen chopped okra, thawed

1. Spray 4-quart Dutch oven with cooking spray; heat over medium heat until hot. Add onion, bell pepper, celery and garlic. Cook and stir 3 minutes or until crisp-tender.

2. Add stewed tomatoes, juice, beans, parsley, oregano, pepper sauce and bay leaves. Bring to a boil over high heat. Add rice. Cover; reduce heat to medium-low. Simmer 15 minutes or until rice is tender.

3. Add okra; cook, covered, 5 minutes more or until okra is tender. Remove bay leaves; discard.

Makes 4 (2-cup) servings

Hearty Vegetable Gumbo

Velveeta® Cheesy Broccoli Soup

Prep Time: 10 minutes
Cook Time: 15 minutes

¼ cup chopped onion
1 tablespoon butter or margarine
1½ cups milk
¾ pound (12 ounces) VELVEETA® Pasteurized Prepared Cheese Product, cut up
1 package (10 ounces) frozen chopped broccoli, thawed, drained
Dash pepper

1. Cook and stir onion in butter in large saucepan on medium-high heat until tender.

2. Add remaining ingredients; stir on low heat until VELVEETA is melted and soup is thoroughly heated.

Makes 4 (¾-cup) servings

Use Your Microwave: Microwave onion and butter in 2-quart microwaveable casserole or bowl on HIGH 30 seconds to 1 minute or until onion is tender. Add remaining ingredients; mix well. Microwave 6 to 8 minutes or until VELVEETA is melted and soup is thoroughly heated, stirring every 3 minutes.

Velveeta® Cheesy Broccoli Soup

Cheesy Potato Chowder

1½ cups water
3 medium red potatoes, peeled and cubed
1 rib celery, sliced
1 medium carrot, chopped
¼ cup butter or margarine
3 green onions, sliced
¼ cup all-purpose flour
1 teaspoon salt
⅛ teaspoon black pepper
4 cups milk
2 cups (8 ounces) shredded American cheese
1 cup (4 ounces) shredded Swiss cheese
½ teaspoon caraway seeds
Oyster crackers (optional)
Fresh chervil for garnish

1. Combine water, potatoes, celery and carrot in medium saucepan. Bring to a boil over high heat. Reduce heat to medium; simmer, uncovered, 10 minutes or until vegetables are tender.

2. Meanwhile, melt butter in large saucepan over medium heat. Cook and stir onions in butter 2 minutes or until onions are tender but not brown. Stir in flour, salt and pepper. Cook and stir about 1 minute.

3. Stir milk and potato mixture into flour mixture; cook and stir over medium heat until bubbly. Cook and stir 1 minute more. Stir in cheeses and caraway seeds. Reduce heat to low; simmer, uncovered, until cheeses are melted and mixture is hot, stirring constantly. Garnish with chervil. Serve with oyster crackers, if desired.

Makes 6 servings

Pasta with Four Cheeses

¾ cup uncooked ziti or rigatoni
3 tablespoons butter, divided
½ cup grated CUCINA CLASSICA ITALIANA® Parmesan cheese, divided
¼ teaspoon ground nutmeg, divided
¼ cup GALBANI® Mascarpone
¾ cup (about 3½ ounces) shredded mozzarella cheese
¾ cup (about 3½ ounces) shredded BEL PAESE® semi-soft cheese

Preheat oven to 350°F. Lightly grease 1-quart casserole. Set aside.

In large saucepan of boiling water, cook pasta until tender but still firm. Drain in colander. Place in large mixing bowl. Stir in 1½ tablespoons butter, ¼ cup Parmesan cheese and ⅛ teaspoon nutmeg.

Spread one fourth of pasta mixture into prepared casserole. Spoon Mascarpone onto pasta. Layer with one fourth of pasta. Top with mozzarella. Add third layer of pasta. Sprinkle with Bel Paese® cheese. Top with remaining pasta. Dot with remaining 1½ tablespoons butter. Sprinkle with remaining ¼ cup Parmesan cheese and ⅛ teaspoon nutmeg. Bake until golden brown, about 20 minutes. *Makes 4 servings*

Roasted Vegetables with Fettuccine

2 pounds assorted fresh vegetables*
1 envelope LIPTON® RECIPE SECRETS® Garlic Mushroom Soup Mix**
3 tablespoons olive or vegetable oil
½ cup light cream, whipping or heavy cream or half-and-half
¼ cup grated Parmesan cheese
8 ounces fettuccine or linguine, cooked and drained

**Use any of the following vegetables, cut into 1-inch chunks: red, green or yellow bell peppers, zucchini, yellow squash, red onion or eggplant.*

***Also terrific with LIPTON® RECIPE SECRETS® Golden Onion or Fiesta Herb with Red Pepper Soup Mix.*

Preheat oven to 450°F.

In large plastic bag or bowl, combine vegetables, garlic mushroom soup mix and oil. Close bag and shake, or toss in bowl, until vegetables are evenly coated. In 13×9-inch baking or roasting pan, arrange vegetables; discard bag.

Bake uncovered, stirring once, 20 minutes or until vegetables are tender. Stir in light cream and cheese until evenly coated. Toss with hot fettuccine. Serve, if desired, with additional grated Parmesan cheese and freshly ground black pepper.

Makes about 2 main-dish or 4 side-dish servings

Gnocchi with BelGioioso Gorgonzola

2 pounds potatoes, peeled
2⅓ cups flour
1 egg
Salt to taste
1 cup BELGIOIOSO® Gorgonzola, cut into cubes
1 tablespoon water
Black pepper to taste

Boil peeled potatoes; mash. Add flour, egg and salt to potatoes; mix by hand until dough is soft and compact. With floured hands, make small potato rolls (about 1-inch long). Drop into boiling water; cook in batches about 2 minutes. Remove gnocchi with slotted spoon. Meanwhile, cut BelGioioso Gorgonzola into cubes; melt in pan over low heat. Add water and pepper. Toss cooked gnocchi with Gorgonzola sauce; serve.

Makes 6 servings

Roasted Vegetables with Fettuccine

Orzotto with Herbs and Mushrooms

1 medium onion, chopped
2 tablespoons minced garlic
4 tablespoons olive oil
1 package (16 ounces) BARILLA® Orzo
3 cups chicken broth
1¾ cups (4 ounces) assorted mushrooms, sliced
½ cup red bell pepper, finely chopped
½ cup green bell pepper, finely chopped
½ cup yellow bell pepper, finely chopped
1 tablespoon dried Italian seasoning
½ cup white wine
⅓ cup heavy whipping cream
4 ounces herbed cheese spread, at room temperature
1 (4-ounce) piece prosciutto ham, diced
Salt and pepper
Grated Parmesan cheese

1. Cook onion and garlic in olive oil in Dutch oven or large pot over medium heat until onion is transparent.

2. Add orzo to Dutch oven; cook and stir 1 minute. Add chicken broth; heat to boiling. Reduce heat to low; cook about 7 to 8 minutes, stirring frequently, until orzo is tender but still firm. Add mushrooms, peppers and Italian seasoning; cook over medium heat, stirring frequently, until pasta and vegetables are just tender.

3. Stir in wine, cream and herbed cheese. Cook over low heat until smooth, stirring constantly. Stir in prosciutto; add salt and pepper to taste.

4. Remove from heat; cover and let stand 5 minutes. Serve with cheese.

Makes 8 to 10 servings

Orzotto with Herbs and Mushrooms

Pasta and Broccoli

1 bunch broccoli
1 package (16 ounces) uncooked ziti macaroni
2 tablespoons olive oil
1 clove garlic, minced
¾ cup (3 ounces) shredded American or mozzarella cheese
½ cup grated Parmesan cheese
¼ cup butter
¼ cup chicken broth
3 tablespoons white wine

1. Cut broccoli into florets. Peel stalks, then cut into 1-inch pieces.

2. To steam broccoli, bring 2 inches of water in large saucepan to a boil over high heat. Place broccoli in metal steamer into saucepan. Water should not touch broccoli. Cover pan; steam 10 minutes until broccoli is tender. Add water, as necessary, to prevent pan from boiling dry.

3. Cook pasta according to package directions. Drain in colander.

4. Heat oil in large skillet over medium-high heat. Cook and stir garlic in hot oil until golden.

5. Add broccoli; cook and stir 3 to 4 minutes. Add American cheese, Parmesan cheese, butter, broth and wine; stir. Reduce heat to low. Simmer until cheese melts.

6. Pour sauce over ziti in large bowl; toss gently to coat. Garnish as desired.

Makes 6 to 8 servings

Pasta and Broccoli

Potatoes au Gratin

4 to 6 medium unpeeled baking potatoes (about 2 pounds)
2 cups (8 ounces) shredded Cheddar cheese
1 cup (4 ounces) shredded Swiss cheese
2 tablespoons butter or margarine
3 tablespoons all-purpose flour
2½ cups milk
2 tablespoons Dijon mustard
¼ teaspoon salt
¼ teaspoon black pepper

1. Preheat oven to 400°F. Grease 13×9-inch baking dish.

2. Cut potatoes into thin slices. Layer potatoes in prepared dish. Top with cheeses.

3. Melt butter in medium saucepan over medium heat. Stir in flour; cook 1 minute. Stir in milk, mustard, salt and pepper; bring to a boil. Reduce heat and cook, stirring constantly, until mixture thickens. Pour milk mixture over cheese. Cover pan with foil.

4. Bake 30 minutes. Remove foil and bake 15 to 20 minutes more until potatoes are tender and top is brown. Remove from oven and let stand 10 minutes before serving.

Makes 6 to 8 servings

Creamed Spinach

Prep Time: 5 minutes
Cook Time: 10 minutes

2 cups milk
1 package KNORR® Recipe Classics™ Leek Soup, Dip and Recipe Mix
1 bag (16 ounces) frozen chopped spinach
⅛ teaspoon ground nutmeg

• In medium saucepan, combine milk and recipe mix. Bring to a boil over medium heat.

• Add spinach and nutmeg. Bring to a boil over high heat, stirring frequently. Reduce heat to low and simmer, stirring frequently, 5 minutes.

Makes 6 servings

Potatoes au Gratin

Georgia-Style Lemon Pilaf

¼ cup WESSON® Vegetable Oil
½ cup minced sweet onion
½ cup diced celery
1 cup uncooked long-grain rice
1 (14½-ounce) can chicken broth
½ cup water
⅓ cup dried currants
2 tablespoons fresh lemon juice
2 teaspoons grated fresh lemon peel
¼ cup sliced almonds, toasted
1 tablespoon fresh chopped parsley

In a large saucepan, heat Wesson® Oil until hot. Add onion and celery; sauté until crisp-tender. Add rice; continue sautéing an additional 3 minutes. Mix in *remaining* ingredients *except* almonds and parsley. Bring mixture to a boil, stirring occasionally. Cover; reduce heat to medium-low and cook until liquid is absorbed and rice is tender, about 20 minutes. Mix in almonds and parsley; cover and let stand 5 minutes. Fluff with fork before serving. *Makes 4 servings*

Hidden Valley® Glazed Baby Carrots

¼ cup butter
¼ cup packed light brown sugar
1 package (16 ounces) ready-to-eat baby carrots, cooked
1 packet (1 ounce) HIDDEN VALLEY® Original Ranch® Salad Dressing & Seasoning Mix

Melt butter and sugar in a large skillet. Add carrots and salad dressing & seasoning mix; stir well. Cook over medium heat until carrots are heated through and glazed, about 5 minutes, stirring frequently. *Makes 4 to 6 servings*

Georgia-Style Lemon Pilaf

Layered Pear Cream Cheese Mold

Preparation Time: 30 minutes
Refrigerating Time: 5 hours

- **1 can (16 ounces) pear halves, undrained**
- **1 package (8-serving size) *or* 2 packages (4-serving size) JELL-O® Brand Lime Flavor Gelatin Dessert**
- **1½ cups cold ginger ale or water**
- **2 tablespoons lemon juice**
- **1 package (8 ounces) PHILADELPHIA® Cream Cheese, softened**
- **¼ cup chopped pecans**

DRAIN pears, reserving liquid. Dice pears; set aside. Add water to liquid to make 1½ cups; bring to boil in small saucepan.

STIR boiling liquid into gelatin in large bowl at least 2 minutes until completely dissolved. Stir in cold ginger ale and lemon juice. Reserve 2½ cups gelatin at room temperature. Pour remaining gelatin into 5-cup mold. Refrigerate about 30 minutes or until thickened (spoon drawn through leaves definite impression). Arrange about ½ cup of the diced pears in thickened gelatin in mold. Refrigerate.

STIR reserved 2½ cups gelatin gradually into cream cheese in large bowl with wire whisk until smooth. Refrigerate about 30 minutes or until slightly thickened (consistency of unbeaten egg whites). Stir in remaining diced pears and pecans. Spoon over gelatin layer in mold.

REFRIGERATE 4 hours or until firm. Unmold. Garnish as desired.

Makes 10 servings

Layered Pear Cream Cheese Mold

Original Green Bean Casserole

Prep Time: 5 minutes
Cook Time: 35 minutes

1 can (10¾ ounces) condensed cream of mushroom soup
¾ cup milk
⅛ teaspoon pepper
2 packages (9 ounces each) frozen cut green beans, thawed*
1⅓ cups *French's*® French Fried Onions, divided

**Substitute 2 cans (14½ ounces each) cut green beans, drained, for frozen green beans.*

1. Preheat oven to 350°F. Combine soup, milk and pepper in 1½-quart casserole; stir until well blended. Stir in beans and *⅔ cup* French Fried Onions.

2. Bake, uncovered, 30 minutes or until hot; stir. Sprinkle with remaining *⅔ cup* onions. Bake 5 minutes or until onions are golden brown. *Makes 6 servings*

Microwave Directions: Prepare green bean mixture as above; pour into 1½-quart microwave-safe casserole. Cover with vented plastic wrap. Microwave on HIGH 8 to 10 minutes or until heated through, stirring halfway. Uncover. Top with remaining French Fried Onions. Cook 1 minute until onions are golden. Let stand 5 minutes.

Creamy Broccoli and Cheese

1 package (8 ounces) cream cheese, softened
¾ cup milk
1 packet (1 ounce) HIDDEN VALLEY® Original Ranch® Salad Dressing & Seasoning Mix
1 pound fresh broccoli florets, cooked and drained
½ cup (2 ounces) shredded sharp Cheddar cheese

In a food processor fitted with a metal blade, blend cream cheese, milk and salad dressing & seasoning mix until smooth. Pour over broccoli in a 9-inch baking dish; stir well. Top with cheese. Bake at 350°F for 25 minutes or until cheese is melted.
Makes 4 servings

Eggplant Cheese Casserole

1 package (1.5 ounce) LAWRY'S® Original-Style Spaghetti Sauce Spices & Seasoning
1 can (8 ounce) tomato sauce
1½ cups water
½ cup finely chopped onion
1 teaspoon LAWRY'S® Seasoned Salt
1 large eggplant, peeled and cut into ¼-inch slices
¾ to 1 cup salad oil
½ pound mozzarella cheese, thinly sliced
¼ cup grated Parmesan cheese

In medium saucepan, combine Original-Style Spaghetti Sauce Spices & Seasonings, tomato sauce, water, onion and Seasoned Salt; mix well. Bring to a boil over medium-high heat; reduce heat to low and simmer, uncovered, 20 minutes. In large skillet, heat oil. Add eggplant and cook over medium-high heat until browned, adding oil as needed. Drain eggplant thoroughly on paper towels. Pour ⅓ of sauce into 8-inch square dish. Cover sauce with layers of ½ the eggplant and mozzarella slices. Repeat layers, ending with sauce and top with Parmesan cheese. Bake, uncovered, in 350°F oven 20 minutes. Let stand 10 minutes before cutting into squares.

Makes 6 servings

Serving Suggestion: Serve with a vegetable salad and fruit dessert, or as an accompaniment to roast lamb or grilled lamb chops.

Confetti Scalloped Corn

- 1 egg, beaten
- 1 cup skim milk
- 1 cup coarsely crushed saltine crackers (about 22 two-inch square crackers), divided
- ¼ teaspoon salt
- ⅛ teaspoon pepper
- 1 can (about 16 ounces) cream-style corn
- ¼ cup finely chopped onion
- 1 jar (2 ounces) chopped pimiento, drained
- 1 tablespoon CRISCO® Oil*
- 1 tablespoon chopped fresh parsley

**Use your favorite Crisco Oil product.*

1. Heat oven to 350°F.

2. Combine egg, milk, ⅔ cup cracker crumbs, salt and pepper in medium bowl. Stir in corn, onion and pimiento. Pour into ungreased 1-quart casserole.

3. Combine remaining ⅓ cup cracker crumbs with oil in small bowl. Toss to coat. Sprinkle over corn mixture.

4. Bake at 350°F for 1 hour or until knife inserted in center comes out clean. *Do not overbake.* Sprinkle with parsley. Let stand 5 to 10 minutes before serving. Garnish, if desired.

Makes 6 servings

Confetti Scalloped Corn

Velveeta® Twice Baked Ranch Potatoes

Prep Time: 20 minutes plus baking potatoes
Bake Time: 20 minutes

4 baking potatoes
½ cup KRAFT® Ranch Dressing
¼ cup BREAKSTONE'S® or KNUDSEN® Sour Cream
1 tablespoon OSCAR MAYER® Real Bacon Bits
¼ pound (4 ounces) VELVEETA® Pasteurized Prepared Cheese Product, cut up

1. Bake potatoes at 400°F for 1 hour. Slice off tops of potatoes; scoop out centers, leaving ⅛-inch shells.

2. Mash potatoes. Add dressing, sour cream and bacon bits; beat until fluffy. Stir VELVEETA into potato mixture. Spoon into shells.

3. Bake at 350°F for 20 minutes.

Makes 4 servings

How to Bake Potatoes: Russet potatoes are best for baking. Scrub potatoes well, blot dry and rub the skins with a little oil and salt. Prick the skins of the potatoes with a fork so steam can escape. Stand them on end in a muffin tin. Bake at 400°F for 1 hour or until tender.

Orange Sesame Couscous

1 cup fresh orange juice (3 SUNKIST® oranges)
½ cup chopped red or green bell pepper
1 teaspoon sesame oil
⅛ teaspoon salt
⅔ cup uncooked couscous
1 SUNKIST® orange, peeled and cut into bite-size pieces
3 tablespoons chopped green onions

In medium saucepan, combine orange juice, bell pepper, sesame oil and salt. Bring just to a boil; stir in couscous. Cover and remove from heat. Let stand 5 minutes. Stir with fork to fluff up mixture. Stir in orange pieces and green onions.

Makes 3 (1-cup) servings

Velveeta® Twice Baked Ranch Potatoes

Grated Potato and Blue Cheese Casserole

2 teaspoons butter or margarine
1½ cups finely chopped red onions
8 ounces Neufchâtel cheese, softened
¼ to ⅓ cup finely crumbled domestic blue cheese
¾ cup heavy cream
1 tablespoon minced fresh thyme *or* 1 teaspoon dried thyme leaves
½ teaspoon salt
2 pounds baking potatoes (about 4 medium)
Fresh thyme sprigs and red pearl onion wedges for garnish

1. Preheat oven to 350°F. Grease 11×7-inch broilerproof baking dish; set aside.

2. Melt butter in large skillet over medium heat; add onions. Cook and stir about 5 minutes or until onions are softened and translucent. Remove onions from skillet to small bowl; set aside to cool.

3. Beat Neufchâtel cheese in large bowl with electric mixer at medium speed until fluffy. Add blue cheese; beat until blended. Beat in cream, thyme and salt at low speed until mixture is fairly smooth. (There will be some small lumps.) Add cooled onions; beat until blended. Set aside.

4. Peel potatoes, then grate 1 potato into cheese mixture with large-holed section of metal grater. Fold into cheese mixture with rubber spatula (this prevents potato from turning brown). Repeat with remaining potatoes, 1 at a time.

5. Pour mixture into prepared baking dish; cover with foil. Bake 45 minutes. Uncover; bake 15 to 20 minutes more until crisp around edges.

6. Turn oven to broil. Broil casserole, 6 inches from heat, 3 to 5 minutes until top is golden brown.

7. Remove from oven; let stand 5 minutes before serving. Garnish, if desired.

Makes 6 servings

Grated Potato and Blue Cheese Casserole

Southwestern Rice

1 cup uncooked converted rice
1 can (15 ounces) black beans, rinsed and drained
1 can (8 ounces) corn, drained
1 packet (1 ounce) HIDDEN VALLEY® Original Ranch® Salad Dressing & Seasoning Mix
¾ cup (3 ounces) diced Monterey Jack cheese
½ cup seeded, diced tomato
¼ cup sliced green onions

Cook rice according to package directions, omitting salt. During last five minutes of cooking time, quickly uncover and add beans and corn; cover immediately. When rice is done, remove saucepan from heat; add salad dressing & seasoning mix and stir. Let stand, covered, 5 minutes. Stir in cheese, tomato and onions. Serve immediately.

Makes 6 servings

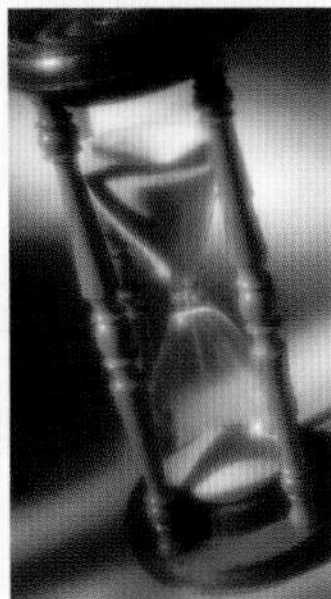

Quick Tip

Regular long-grain rice may be substituted for the converted rice in this Tex-Mex inspired side dish. Just cook it according to package directions, being sure to omit the salt.

Southwestern Rice

Southern Spoon Bread

4 eggs, separated
3 cups milk
1 cup yellow cornmeal
3 tablespoons margarine or butter
1 teaspoon salt
¼ teaspoon black pepper *or* ⅛ teaspoon ground red pepper
1 teaspoon baking powder
1 tablespoon grated Parmesan cheese (optional)

1. Preheat oven to 375°F. Spray 2-quart round casserole with nonstick cooking spray; set aside. Beat egg yolks in small bowl; set aside.

2. Heat milk almost to a boil in medium saucepan over medium heat. Gradually beat in cornmeal using wire whisk. Cook 2 minutes, stirring constantly. Whisk in margarine, salt and pepper. Beat about ¼ cup cornmeal mixture into egg yolks. Beat egg yolk mixture into remaining cornmeal mixture; set aside.

3. Beat egg whites in large bowl with electric mixer at high speed until stiff peaks form. Stir baking powder into cornmeal mixture. Stir about ¼ cup egg whites into cornmeal mixture. Gradually fold in remaining egg whites. Pour into prepared casserole; sprinkle with cheese, if desired.

4. Bake 30 to 35 minutes or until golden brown and toothpick inserted into center comes out clean. Serve immediately.

Makes 6 servings

Southern Spoon Bread

Wild Rice and Dried Fruit Pilaf

2 cups chicken broth
1 cup uncooked California wild rice, rinsed
1 tablespoon butter
1 onion, sliced into thin wedges
2 teaspoons firmly packed brown sugar
¼ cup golden raisins
¼ cup dried cranberries or cherries
¼ cup chopped dried apricots
1 teaspoon grated orange zest
Juice from 1 orange
¼ teaspoon black pepper
2 tablespoons chopped parsley

Combine chicken broth and wild rice in medium saucepan; bring to a boil. Reduce heat; cover and simmer 40 minutes or until almost tender.

Melt butter in small saucepan over low heat; stir in onion and brown sugar. Cook 10 minutes, stirring occasionally, until onion is tender and lightly browned.

Add cooked onion, raisins, cranberries, apricots, orange zest, orange juice and pepper to rice mixture. Cover and simmer 10 minutes or until rice is tender and grains have puffed open. Stir in parsley. *Makes 6 servings*

Favorite recipe from *California Wild Rice Advisory Board*

The Original Ranch® Roasted Potatoes

2 pounds small red potatoes, quartered
¼ cup vegetable oil
1 packet (1 ounce) HIDDEN VALLEY® The Original Ranch® Salad Dressing & Seasoning Mix

Place potatoes in a resealable plastic bag and add oil; seal bag. Toss to coat. Add salad dressing & seasoning mix and toss again until coated. Bake in an ungreased baking pan at 450°F for 35 minutes or until potatoes are brown and crisp.

Makes 4 to 6 servings

Wisconsin Romano and Roasted Garlic Mashed Potatoes

½ cup olive oil
15 cloves garlic, peeled
10 medium baking potatoes, peeled
1 cup milk
½ cup grated Wisconsin Romano cheese
½ cup butter
Salt and black pepper to taste

Place olive oil and garlic in small pan and simmer slowly until garlic is browned. Purée garlic and oil; reserve. Cut potatoes into medium-sized chunks. Place in large saucepan or Dutch oven; cover with cold water. Bring to a boil. Cook until potatoes are just tender. Strain off all water and return potatoes to pot. Add all ingredients including olive oil/garlic purée; mash potatoes by hand until smooth. Garnish servings with additional grated romano cheese and chopped parsley, if desired.

Makes 10 servings

Favorite recipe from *Wisconsin Milk Marketing Board*

Cinnamon Apple Sweet Potatoes

4 medium sweet potatoes
1½ cups finely chopped apples
½ cup orange juice
¼ cup sugar
1½ teaspoons cornstarch
½ teaspoon ground cinnamon
½ teaspoon grated orange peel

Microwave Directions

Prick potatoes with fork. Place on paper towels and microwave at HIGH (100%) 10 to 13 minutes or until tender, turning halfway through cooking. Set aside. In microwavable bowl, combine remaining ingredients. Cover and microwave 3 minutes; stir. Microwave uncovered 1½ to 2½ minutes or until sauce is thickened. Slit sweet potatoes and spoon sauce over each.

Makes 4 servings

Tip: Sauce can be made ahead, covered, refrigerated and reheated.

Favorite recipe from *The Sugar Association, Inc.*

Rice Pilaf with Dried Cherries and Almonds

½ cup slivered almonds
2 tablespoons margarine
2 cups uncooked converted rice
½ cup chopped onion
1 can (about 14 ounces) chicken broth
1½ cups water
½ cup dried cherries

1. Cook and stir almonds in large nonstick skillet over medium heat until lightly browned. Remove from skillet; cool.

2. Melt margarine in skillet over low heat. Add rice and onion; cook and stir until rice is lightly browned. Add broth and water. Bring to a boil over high heat; reduce heat to low. Simmer, covered, 15 minutes.

3. Stir in almonds and cherries. Simmer 5 minutes or until liquid is absorbed and rice is tender.

Makes 12 servings

Broccoli-Cheese Casserole

1 package (10 ounces) frozen chopped broccoli, thawed and drained
1 package (1 ounce) HIDDEN VALLEY® The Original Ranch® Salad Dressing & Seasoning Mix
1 cup (½ pint) sour cream
1 cup milk
½ cup shredded Monterey Jack cheese
¼ cup seasoned bread crumbs (optional)
1 tablespoon butter or margarine, melted (optional)

Preheat oven to 350°F. Place broccoli in greased shallow baking dish. In medium bowl, whisk together salad dressing & seasoning mix, sour cream and milk. Drizzle ¾ cup dressing mixture over broccoli (reserve remaining dressing for another use). Top with cheese. Cover loosely with foil. Bake until heated through, 15 to 20 minutes. If desired, combine bread crumbs and butter. Sprinkle on top of casserole during last 5 minutes of baking; do not cover with foil.

Makes 6 servings

Rice Pilaf with Dried Cherries and Almonds

Ranch Picnic Potato Salad

6 medium potatoes (about 3½ pounds), cooked, peeled and sliced
½ cup chopped celery
¼ cup sliced green onions
2 tablespoons chopped parsley
1 teaspoon salt
⅛ teaspoon black pepper
1 cup HIDDEN VALLEY® Original Ranch® Dressing
1 tablespoon Dijon mustard
2 hard-cooked eggs, finely chopped
Paprika
Lettuce (optional)

Combine potatoes, celery, onions, parsley, salt and pepper in a large bowl. Stir together dressing and mustard in a small bowl; pour over potato mixture and toss lightly. Cover and refrigerate several hours. Sprinkle with eggs and paprika. Serve in a lettuce-lined bowl, if desired. *Makes 8 servings*

Chunky Applesauce

10 tart apples (about 3 pounds) peeled, cored and chopped
¾ cup packed light brown sugar
½ cup apple juice or apple cider
1½ teaspoons ground cinnamon
⅛ teaspoon salt
⅛ teaspoon ground nutmeg

1. Combine apples, brown sugar, apple juice, cinnamon, salt and nutmeg in heavy, large saucepan; cover. Cook over medium-low heat 40 to 45 minutes or until apples are tender, stirring occasionally with wooden spoon to break up apples. Remove saucepan from heat. Cool completely.

2. Store in airtight container in refrigerator up to 1 month. *Makes about 5½ cups*

Ranch Picnic Potato Salad

Strawberry Miracle Mold

Prep Time: 10 minutes plus refrigerating

1½ cups boiling water
2 packages (4-serving size) JELL-O® Brand Strawberry Flavor Gelatin
1¾ cups cold water
½ cup MIRACLE WHIP® Salad Dressing
Assorted fruit

Stir boiling water into gelatin in medium bowl 2 minutes or until dissolved. Stir in cold water. Gradually whisk gelatin into salad dressing in large bowl until well blended.

Pour into 1-quart mold or glass serving bowl that has been lightly sprayed with non-stick cooking spray. Refrigerate until firm. Unmold onto serving plate; serve with fruit.

Makes 4 to 6 servings

Cheesy Vegetable Casserole

Prep Time: 5 minutes
Cook Time: 35 minutes

1 can (10¾ ounces) condensed Cheddar cheese soup
2 cups shredded Cheddar cheese
½ cup sour cream
¼ cup milk
1 bag (16 ounces) frozen vegetable combination, thawed and drained
1½ cups *French's*® French Fried Onions

1. Preheat oven to 350°F. Combine soup, *1 cup* cheese, sour cream and milk in 2-quart baking dish. Stir in vegetables.

2. Bake, uncovered, 30 minutes or until hot; stir.

3. Top with remaining *1 cup* cheese and French Fried Onions. Bake 5 minutes or until golden.

Makes 6 servings

Microwave Directions: Prepare vegetable mixture as above in microwave-safe baking dish. Cover with vented plastic wrap. Microwave on HIGH 10 minutes or until hot, stirring halfway. Top with cheese and French Fried Onions. Microwave 2 minutes or until golden.

Strawberry Miracle Mold

Curry Pasta Salad

- 6 ounces uncooked small shell pasta
- 1 container (6 to 8 ounces) lemon nonfat or low-fat yogurt
- 2 tablespoons fresh lime juice
- ¾ teaspoon curry powder
- ¼ teaspoon salt
- ⅛ teaspoon black pepper
- 1 medium-size ripe mango, peeled and cut into ½-inch pieces
- 1 small red bell pepper, chopped
- 1 to 2 green onions, thinly sliced
- 2 tablespoons chopped fresh cilantro leaves
- 2 tablespoons chopped peanuts
- Lime wedges (optional)

1. Prepare pasta according to package directions; drain well and set aside. Meanwhile, combine yogurt, lime juice, curry powder, salt and black pepper in medium bowl. Add pasta and stir until evenly coated with dressing.

2. Spoon mango over pasta. Top with bell pepper, onion and cilantro; sprinkle with peanuts. Serve with lime wedges, if desired. *Makes 6 servings*

Note: This salad can be prepared ahead of time and refrigerated.

Philadelphia® Creamy Mashed Potatoes

Prep Time: 30 minutes

- 2½ pounds potatoes, peeled and quartered
- 1 package (8 ounces) PHILADELPHIA® Cream Cheese Spread
- 1 tablespoon butter or margarine
- 1 teaspoon salt

COOK potatoes in boiling water in large saucepan 20 minutes or until tender. Drain.

BEAT potatoes with electric mixer on medium speed 1 minute. Add remaining ingredients; beat until smooth. *Makes 8 servings*

Variation: Prepare as directed, using PHILADELPHIA® Chive & Onion Cream Cheese Spread.

Curry Pasta Salad

Mediterranean Strata

Prep Time: 15 minutes
Cook Time: about 1 hour

2 pounds green zucchini or yellow squash, cut into ¼-inch slices
1 cup ricotta cheese
3 eggs
1½ cups milk, heavy cream or half-and-half cream
1 cup minced fresh basil (2 bunches)
2 tablespoons all-purpose flour
1 tablespoon minced garlic
1 cup shredded mozzarella cheese
1 cup *French's*® French Fried Onions

1. Preheat oven to 350°F. Place zucchini and *2 tablespoons water* into 2-quart microwave-safe baking dish. Cover with vented plastic wrap. Microwave on HIGH 3 minutes or until just tender; drain well.

2. Whisk together ricotta cheese, eggs, milk, basil, flour, garlic and *½ teaspoon salt* in large bowl. Pour over zucchini. Bake, uncovered, 50 minutes or until custard is just set.

3. Sprinkle with mozzarella cheese and French Fried Onions. Bake 5 minutes until onions are golden. Garnish with diced red bell pepper, if desired.

Makes 6 servings

Tip: You may substitute 8 ounces crumbled feta cheese for the ricotta cheese. Omit salt.

Mediterranean Strata

Velveeta® Cheesy Rice & Broccoli

Prep Time: 5 minutes
Cook Time: 10 minutes plus standing

1 package (10 ounces) frozen chopped broccoli, thawed, drained
1 cup water
1½ cups MINUTE® White Rice, uncooked
½ pound (8 ounces) VELVEETA® Pasteurized Prepared Cheese Product, cut up

1. Bring broccoli and water to full boil in medium saucepan on medium-high heat.

2. Stir in rice; cover. Remove from heat. Let stand 5 minutes.

3. Add VELVEETA; stir until VELVEETA is melted. *Makes 6 servings*

Garlic Mashed Potatoes

6 medium all-purpose potatoes, peeled, if desired, and cut into chunks (about 3 pounds)
Water
1 envelope LIPTON® RECIPE SECRETS® Savory Herb with Garlic Soup Mix*
½ cup milk
½ cup I CAN'T BELIEVE IT'S NOT BUTTER!® Spread

**Also terrific with LIPTON® RECIPE SECRETS® Onion Mushroom, Onion or Golden Onion Soup Mix.*

In 4-quart saucepan, cover potatoes with water; bring to a boil over high heat.

Reduce heat to low and simmer, uncovered, 20 minutes or until potatoes are very tender; drain.

Return potatoes to saucepan, then mash. Stir in remaining ingredients.

Makes about 8 servings

Velveeta® Cheesy Rice & Broccoli

Pear Couscous Salad

Herb Dressing (recipe follows)
¾ cup chicken broth
½ cup uncooked couscous
1 teaspoon lemon juice
1 Northwest pear, cored and diced
½ cup chopped green bell pepper
2 tablespoons chopped filberts or hazelnuts
1 tablespoon chopped fresh parsley
Salt and black pepper to taste
1 Northwest pear, cored and sliced
4 ounces sliced Jarlsberg or Swiss cheese
Lettuce

Prepare Herb Dressing. In small saucepan, bring broth to a boil. Add couscous and lemon juice; cover and let stand 5 minutes or until couscous is tender and all liquid is absorbed. Toss with 2 tablespoons Herb Dressing; cool. Add diced pear, bell pepper, filberts, parsley and additional dressing to taste. Season with salt and black pepper. Arrange couscous-pear salad, pear slices and cheese on lettuce-lined plates.

Makes 4 servings

Herb Dressing: Combine ¼ cup white wine vinegar, 2 tablespoons olive oil, 1 teaspoon Dijon mustard, 1 teaspoon *each* chopped fresh basil and thyme,* ½ teaspoon sugar, ¼ teaspoon salt and dash black pepper; mix well. Makes about ⅓ cup.

**One-fourth to ½ teaspoon each dried crushed basil and thyme may be substituted.*

Favorite recipe from *Pear Bureau Northwest*

Pear Couscous Salad

Cinnamon Chip Filled Crescents

2 cans (8 ounces each) refrigerated quick crescent dinner rolls
2 tablespoons butter or margarine, melted
1⅔ cups (10-ounce package) HERSHEY'®S Cinnamon Chips, divided
Cinnamon Chips Drizzle (recipe follows)

1. Heat oven to 375°F. Unroll dough; separate into 16 triangles.

2. Spread melted butter on each triangle. Sprinkle 1 cup cinnamon chips evenly over triangles; gently press chips into dough. Roll from shortest side of triangle to opposite point. Place, point side down, on ungreased cookie sheet; curve into crescent shape.

3. Bake 8 to 10 minutes or until golden brown. Drizzle with Cinnamon Chips Drizzle. Serve warm.

Makes 16 crescents

Cinnamon Chips Drizzle: Place remaining ⅔ cup chips and 1½ teaspoons shortening (do not use butter, margarine, spread or oil) in small microwave-safe bowl. Microwave at HIGH (100%) 1 minute; stir until chips are melted.

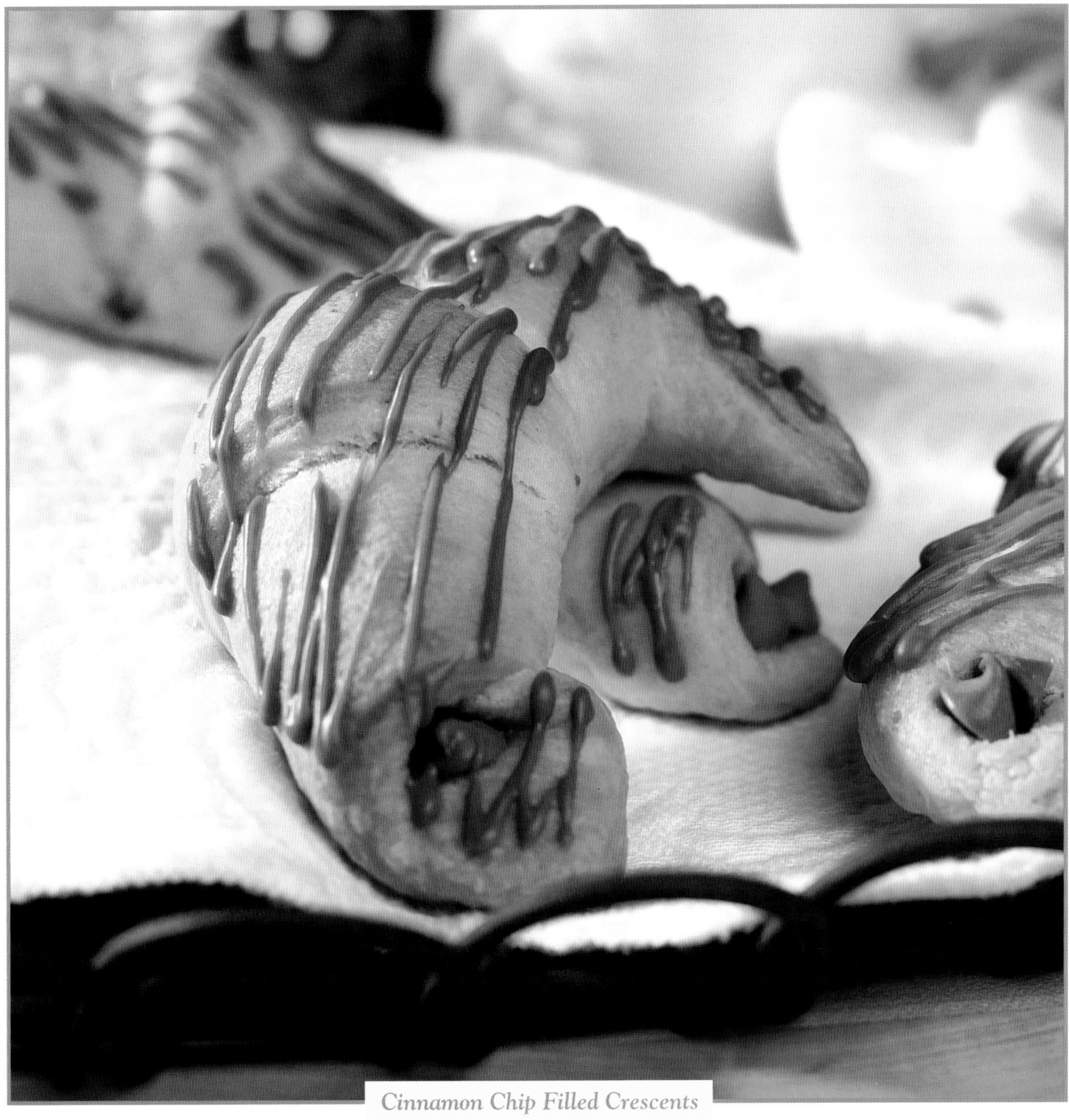
Cinnamon Chip Filled Crescents

Chocolate Chunk Banana Bread

Prep: 15 minutes
Bake: 55 minutes

2 eggs, lightly beaten
1 cup mashed ripe bananas
⅓ cup oil
¼ cup milk
2 cups flour
1 cup sugar
2 teaspoons CALUMET® Baking Powder
¼ teaspoon salt
1 package (4 ounces) BAKER'S® GERMAN'S® Sweet Baking Chocolate, coarsely chopped
½ cup chopped nuts

HEAT oven to 350°F.

STIR eggs, bananas, oil and milk until well blended. Add flour, sugar, baking powder and salt; stir until just moistened. Stir in chocolate and nuts. Pour into greased 9×5-inch loaf pan.

BAKE for 55 minutes or until toothpick inserted into center comes out clean. Cool in pan 10 minutes. Remove from pan; cool completely on wire rack.

Makes 18 (½-inch) servings

Note: For easier slicing, wrap bread and store overnight.

Bottom to top: Chocolate Chunk Banana Bread and Chocolate Chunk Sour Cream Muffins (page 214)

Chocolate Chunk Sour Cream Muffins

Prep: 15 minutes
Bake: 30 minutes

½ cup milk
2 tablespoons MAXWELL HOUSE® Instant Coffee, any variety
1½ cups flour
½ cup sugar
1½ teaspoons CALUMET® Baking Powder
½ teaspoon cinnamon
¼ teaspoon salt
2 eggs
½ cup BREAKSTONE'S® Sour Cream or plain yogurt
¼ cup (½ stick) butter or margarine, melted
1 teaspoon vanilla
1 package (4 ounces) BAKER'S® GERMAN'S® Sweet Baking Chocolate, chopped

HEAT oven to 375°F.

STIR milk and instant coffee in small bowl until well blended; set aside. Mix flour, sugar, baking powder, cinnamon and salt in large bowl. Beat eggs in small bowl; stir in coffee-milk mixture, sour cream, butter and vanilla until well blended. Add flour mixture; stir just until moistened. Stir in chopped chocolate.

SPOON batter into greased or paper-lined muffin pan, filling each cup ⅔ full.

BAKE for 30 minutes or until toothpick inserted into center comes out clean. Serve warm.

Makes 12 muffins

Raspberry Breakfast Braid

Coffee Cake

2 cups packaged baking mix
1 (3-ounce) package cream cheese
¼ cup butter or margarine
⅓ cup milk
½ cup SMUCKER'S® Red Raspberry Preserves

Glaze

1 cup powdered sugar
¼ teaspoon almond extract
¼ teaspoon vanilla
1 to 2 tablespoons milk

In medium bowl, measure baking mix. Cut in cream cheese and butter until mixture is crumbly. Stir in milk. Turn dough onto a lightly floured surface and knead lightly 10 to 12 times. Roll dough into a 12×8-inch rectangle. Turn onto greased baking sheet. Spread preserves lengthwise down center ⅓ of dough. Make 2½-inch cuts at 1-inch intervals on long sides. Fold strips over filling.

Bake at 425°F for 12 to 15 minutes or until lightly browned.

Combine all glaze ingredients, adding enough milk for desired drizzling consistency. Drizzle over coffee cake. *Makes 10 to 12 servings*

Garlic Bread

¼ cup (½ stick) butter or margarine, softened
⅛ teaspoon garlic powder
½ loaf French bread, sliced in half lengthwise

In small bowl, combine butter and garlic powder. Spread over cut sides of French bread. Bake at 450°F until lightly browned, about 4 minutes. *Makes 4 servings*

Original Ranch® & Cheddar Bread

1 cup HIDDEN VALLEY® Original Ranch® Dressing
2 cups (8 ounces) shredded sharp Cheddar cheese
1 whole loaf (1 pound) French bread (not sourdough)

Stir together dressing and cheese. Cut bread in half lengthwise. Place on a broiler pan and spread dressing mixture evenly over cut side of each half. Broil until lightly brown. Cut each half into 8 pieces. *Makes 16 pieces*

Baked Banana Doughnuts

2 ripe bananas, mashed
2 egg whites
1 tablespoon vegetable oil
1 cup packed brown sugar
1½ cups all-purpose flour
¾ cup whole wheat flour
2 teaspoons baking powder
½ teaspoon baking soda
¼ teaspoon pumpkin pie spice
1 tablespoon granulated sugar
2 tablespoons chopped walnuts (optional)

Preheat oven to 425°F. Spray baking sheet with nonstick cooking spray. Beat bananas, egg whites, oil and brown sugar in large bowl or food processor. Add flours, baking powder, baking soda and pumpkin pie spice. Mix until well blended. Let stand for 5 minutes for dough to rise. Scoop out heaping tablespoonfuls of dough onto prepared baking sheet. Using thin rubber spatula or butter knife, round out doughnut hole in center of dough (if dough sticks to knife or spatula spray with cooking spray). With spatula, smooth outside edges of dough into round doughnut shape. Repeat until all dough is used. Sprinkle with granulated sugar and walnuts, if desired. Bake 6 to 10 minutes or until tops are golden. *Makes about 22 doughnuts*

Variation: Use 8 ounces solid pack pumpkin instead of bananas to make pumpkin doughnuts.

Favorite recipe from *The Sugar Association, Inc.*

Original Ranch® & Cheddar Bread

Fudgey Peanut Butter Chip Muffins

½ cup applesauce
½ cup quick-cooking rolled oats
¼ cup (½ stick) butter or margarine, softened
½ cup granulated sugar
½ cup packed light brown sugar
1 egg
½ teaspoon vanilla extract
¾ cup all-purpose flour
¼ cup HERSHEY'S® Dutch Processed Cocoa or HERSHEY'S® Cocoa
½ teaspoon baking soda
¼ teaspoon ground cinnamon (optional)
1 cup REESE'S® Peanut Butter Chips
Powdered sugar (optional)

1. Heat oven to 350°F. Line muffin cups (2½ inches in diameter) with paper bake cups.

2. Stir together applesauce and oats in small bowl; set aside. In large bowl, beat butter, granulated sugar, brown sugar, egg and vanilla until well blended. Add applesauce mixture; blend well. Stir together flour, cocoa, baking soda and cinnamon, if desired. Add to butter mixture, blending well. Stir in peanut butter chips. Fill muffin cups ¾ full with batter.

3. Bake 22 to 26 minutes or until wooden pick inserted in center comes out almost clean. Cool slightly in pan on wire rack. Sprinkle muffin tops with powdered sugar, if desired. Serve warm. *Makes 12 to 15 muffins*

Fudgey Chocolate Chip Muffins: Omit Peanut Butter Chips. Add 1 cup HERSHEY'S® Semi-Sweet Chocolate Chips.

Fudgey Peanut Butter Chip Muffins

Focaccia

1 cup water
1 tablespoon olive oil, plus additional for brushing
1 teaspoon salt
1 tablespoon sugar
3 cups bread flour
2¼ teaspoons RED STAR® Active Dry Yeast
Suggested toppings: sun-dried tomatoes, grilled bell pepper slices, sautéed onion rings, fresh and dried herbs of any combination, grated hard cheese

Bread Machine Method
Place room temperature ingredients, except toppings, in pan in order listed. Select dough cycle. Check dough consistency after 5 minutes of kneading, making adjustments if necessary.

Hand-Held Mixer Method
Combine yeast, 1 cup flour, sugar and salt. Combine water and 1 tablespoon oil; heat mixture to 120° to 130°F. Combine dry mixture and liquid mixture in mixing bowl on low speed. Beat 2 to 3 minutes on medium speed. By hand, stir in enough remaining flour to make firm dough. Knead on floured surface 5 to 7 minutes or until smooth and elastic. Add additional flour, if necessary.

Stand Mixer Method
Combine yeast, 1 cup flour, sugar and salt. Combine water and 1 tablespoon oil; heat mixture to 120° to 130°F. Combine dry mixture and liquid mixture in mixing bowl with paddle or beaters 4 minutes on medium speed. Gradually add remaining flour and knead with dough hook 5 to 7 minutes or until smooth and elastic. Add additional flour, if necessary.

Rising, Shaping, and Baking
Place dough in lightly oiled bowl and turn to grease top. Cover; let rise until dough doubles in bulk.* Turn dough onto lightly floured surface; punch down to remove air bubbles. On lightly floured surface, shape dough into a ball. Place on greased cookie sheet. Flatten to 14-inch circle. With knife, cut circle in dough about 1 inch from edge, cutting almost through to cookie sheet. Pierce center with fork. Cover; let rise about 15 minutes. Brush with oil and sprinkle with desired toppings. Bake in preheated 375°F oven 25 to 30 minutes or until golden brown. Remove from cookie sheet to cool. Serve warm or cold.

Makes 1 (14-inch) loaf

**Place two fingers into the dough and then remove them. If the holes remain the dough is ripe and ready to punch down.*

Focaccia

Cranberry Orange Ring

2 cups all-purpose flour
1 cup sugar
1½ teaspoons baking powder
1 teaspoon salt
½ teaspoon baking soda
¼ teaspoon ground cloves
1 tablespoon minced orange peel
1 egg, slightly beaten
¾ cup orange juice
2 tablespoons vegetable oil
1 teaspoon vanilla
¼ teaspoon orange extract
1 cup fresh or frozen whole cranberries

1. Preheat oven to 350°F. Grease a 12-cup tube pan and set aside.

2. Combine flour, sugar, baking powder, salt, baking soda and cloves in large bowl. Add orange peel; mix well. Set aside. Combine egg, orange juice, oil, vanilla and orange extract in medium bowl. Beat until well blended. Add orange juice mixture to flour mixture. Stir until just moistened. Gently fold in cranberries. *Do not overmix.*

3. Spread batter evenly in prepared pan. Bake 30 to 35 minutes (35 to 40 minutes if using frozen cranberries) or until toothpick inserted in center of coffee cake comes out clean. Cool in pan on wire rack 15 to 20 minutes. Invert onto serving plate. Serve warm or at room temperature.

Makes 12 servings

Pineapple Carrot Raisin Muffins

1 cup whole wheat flour
¾ cup all-purpose flour
1 tablespoon baking powder
¼ teaspoon salt (optional)
¼ cup firmly packed brown sugar
1½ cups KELLOGG'S® ALL-BRAN® cereal
1 can (8 ounces) crushed unsweetened pineapple, undrained
½ cup unsweetened orange juice
2 egg whites
¼ cup vegetable oil
¾ cup shredded carrots
⅓ cup seedless raisins

1. Stir together flours, baking powder, salt and sugar. Set aside.

2. In large mixing bowl, combine Kellogg's® All-Bran® cereal, pineapple including juice and orange juice. Let stand 2 minutes or until cereal is softened. Add egg whites and oil. Beat well. Stir in carrots and raisins.

3. Add flour mixture, stirring only until combined. Portion batter evenly into twelve 2½-inch muffin cups coated with cooking spray.

4. Bake at 400°F for 25 minutes or until lightly browned. Serve warm.

Makes 12 muffins

Nutty Cinnamon Sticky Buns

Preparation Time: 10 minutes
Cook Time: 25 minutes
Total Time: 35 minutes

⅓ cup margarine or butter
½ cup packed brown sugar
½ cup PLANTERS® Pecans, chopped
1 teaspoon ground cinnamon
1 (17.3-ounce) package refrigerated biscuits (8 large biscuits)

1. Melt margarine or butter in 9-inch round baking pan in 350°F oven.

2. Mix brown sugar, pecans and cinnamon in small bowl; sprinkle over melted margarine or butter in pan. Arrange biscuits in pan with sides touching (biscuits will fit tightly in pan).

3. Bake at 350°F for 25 to 30 minutes or until biscuits are golden brown and center biscuit is fully cooked. Invert pan immediately onto serving plate. Spread any remaining topping from pan on buns. Serve warm. *Makes 8 buns*

Baking Powder Biscuits

2 cups all-purpose flour
2 teaspoons baking powder
1 teaspoon LAWRY'S® Seasoned Salt
8 tablespoons butter, cut into ¼-inch pieces
⅔ cup milk

In medium bowl, combine flour, baking powder and Seasoned Salt; add butter. With fingertips, rub flour mixture and butter together until it resembles coarse meal. Add milk all at once and stir with wooden spoon just long enough to form a smooth soft dough. Gather into a ball; place on floured surface and roll or pat into a circle ½ inch thick. With 2½-inch biscuit cutter, cut into rounds. Arrange on lightly greased baking sheet and bake in 400°F oven 20 minutes until golden brown.

Makes about 1 dozen biscuits

Serving Suggestion: Serve with fried chicken, soup or stew.

Nutty Cinnamon Sticky Buns

Lemony Wheatful Fruit Bread

Prep Time: 10 minutes
Bake Time: 50 minutes

- **½ cup (1 stick) margarine, melted**
- **½ cup fat free milk**
- **2 eggs**
- **Finely grated peel from 1 lemon**
- **2 tablespoons lemon juice**
- **1 cup sugar**
- **2 cups flour**
- **1½ cups POST® SPOON SIZE® Shredded Wheat Cereal, finely crushed**
- **1 teaspoon baking soda**
- **¼ teaspoon ground cinnamon**
- **1 cup dried fruit mix (such as prune, apricot, pear), chopped**

HEAT oven to 350°F. Spray 9×5-inch loaf pan with no stick cooking spray.

MIX margarine, milk, eggs, lemon peel, juice and sugar in large bowl until well blended. Stir in flour, crushed cereal, baking soda and cinnamon until blended. Stir in fruit. Pour into prepared pan.

BAKE 50 minutes or until bread is golden brown and toothpick inserted in center comes out clean. Cool 10 minutes; remove from pan. Cool completely on wire rack. Store wrapped in plastic wrap.

Makes 1 loaf or 12 (¾-inch) slices

Lemony Wheatful Fruit Bread

Quick Cinnamon Sticky Buns

1 cup packed light brown sugar, divided
10 tablespoons butter, softened and divided
1 package (16 ounces) hot roll mix
2 tablespoons granulated sugar
1 cup hot water (120° to 130°F)
1 egg
1⅔ cups (10-ounce package) HERSHEY'®S Cinnamon Chips

1. Lightly grease two 9-inch round baking pans. Combine ½ cup brown sugar and 4 tablespoons softened butter in small bowl with pastry blender; sprinkle mixture evenly on bottom of prepared pans. Set aside.

2. Combine contents of hot roll mix package, including yeast packet, and granulated sugar in large bowl. Using spoon, stir in water, 2 tablespoons butter and egg until dough pulls away from sides of bowl. Turn dough onto lightly floured surface. With lightly floured hands, shape into ball. Knead 5 minutes or until smooth, using additional flour if necessary.

3. To shape: Using lightly floured rolling pin, roll dough into 15×12-inch rectangle. Spread with remaining 4 tablespoons butter. Sprinkle with remaining ½ cup brown sugar and cinnamon chips, pressing lightly into dough. Starting with 12-inch side, roll tightly as for jelly roll; seal edges.

4. Cut into 1-inch-wide slices with floured knife. Arrange 6 slices, cut sides down, in each prepared pan. Cover with towel; let rise in warm place until doubled, about 30 minutes.

5. Heat oven to 350°F. Uncover rolls. Bake 25 to 30 minutes or until golden brown. Cool 2 minutes in pan; with knife, loosen around edges of pan. Invert onto serving plates. Serve warm or at room temperature. *Makes 12 cinnamon buns*

Quick Cinnamon Sticky Buns

Orange Nut Tea Bread

Preparation Time: 10 minutes
Baking Time: 1 hour

WESSON® No-Stick Cooking Spray
4½ cups sifted all-purpose flour
1½ cups sugar
2 tablespoons baking powder
1½ teaspoons salt
1½ cups PETER PAN® Extra Crunchy Peanut Butter
1½ cups milk
2 eggs, room temperature and well beaten
2 tablespoons grated orange peel
Juice from 1 orange
2 teaspoons vanilla

Preheat oven to 350°F. Spray two 9×5-inch loaf pans with Wesson® Cooking Spray. In large bowl, combine flour, sugar, baking powder and salt. Cut in Peter Pan® Peanut Butter with pastry blender or 2 knives until mixture is crumbly; set aside. In medium bowl, stir together milk, eggs, orange rind, juice and vanilla. Combine milk mixture with flour mixture; stir until dry ingredients are moistened. Evenly divide batter into pans. Bake 1 hour or until wooden pick inserted in centers comes out clean. Let rest 15 minutes. Remove from pans to wire racks. Cool. *Makes 2 loaves*

English Lemon Biscuits

1½ cups cake flour*
¼ teaspoon baking soda
½ teaspoon baking powder
½ teaspoon salt
¾ cup granulated sugar
¼ cup nonfat vanilla or plain yogurt
1 egg
2 tablespoons plus 1½ teaspoons vegetable oil
¼ teaspoon finely grated lemon peel
½ teaspoon fresh lemon juice

**Or, substitute 1 cup plus 5 tablespoons all-purpose flour.*

In small bowl, combine flour, baking soda, baking powder and salt; set aside.

In large bowl, combine sugar, yogurt, egg, oil, lemon peel and lemon juice; stir until well blended. Add flour mixture; stir until well blended.

Coat baking sheets with cooking spray. Drop dough by rounded teaspoons 2 inches apart onto baking sheets. Bake in preheated 375°F oven 9 to 12 minutes or until edges are light golden brown. Cool 1 minute; remove from baking sheets and cool on wire racks. *Makes 18 biscuits*

Favorite recipe from *North Dakota Wheat Commission*

Potato Rosemary Rolls

Dough

1 cup plus 2 tablespoons water (70 to 80°F)
2 tablespoons olive oil
1 teaspoon salt
3 cups bread flour
½ cup instant potato flakes or buds
2 tablespoons nonfat dry milk powder
1 tablespoon sugar
1 teaspoon SPICE ISLANDS® Rosemary, crushed
1½ teaspoons FLEISCHMANN'S® Bread Machine Yeast

Topping

1 egg, lightly beaten
SPICE ISLANDS® Sesame or Poppy seed or additional SPICE ISLANDS® Rosemary, crushed

Measure all dough ingredients into bread machine pan in the order suggested by manufacturer, adding potato flakes with flour. Select dough/manual cycle. When cycle is complete, remove dough to floured surface. If necessary, knead in additional flour to make dough easy to handle.

Divide dough into 12 equal pieces. Roll each piece to 10-inch rope; coil each rope and tuck end under coil. Place rolls 2 inches apart on large greased baking sheet. Cover; let rise in warm, draft-free place until doubled in size, about 45 to 60 minutes. Brush tops with beaten egg; sprinkle with sesame seed. Bake at 375°F for 15 to 20 minutes or until rolls are lightly browned and sound hollow when tapped. Remove from pan; cool on wire rack. *Makes 12 rolls*

Note: Dough can be prepared in 1½ and 2-pound capacity bread machines.

Potato Rosemary Rolls

Cranberry-Cheese Batter Bread

1¼ cups milk
3 cups all-purpose flour
½ cup sugar
1 package active dry yeast
1 teaspoon salt
½ cup (1 stick) butter, chilled
½ cup (4 ounces) cream cheese, chilled
1 cup (3-ounce package) dried cranberries

1. Heat milk in small saucepan over low heat until temperature reaches 120° to 130°F. Grease 8-inch square pan; set aside. Combine flour, sugar, yeast and salt in large bowl.

2. Cut butter and cream cheese into 1-inch chunks; add to flour mixture. Cut in butter and cream cheese with pastry blender until mixture resembles coarse crumbs. Add cranberries; toss. Add warm milk; beat 1 minute or until dough looks stringy. Place batter in prepared pan. Cover with towel; let rise in warm place about 1 hour.

3. Preheat oven to 375°F. Bake 35 minutes or until golden brown. *Makes 1 loaf*

Down-home Cornsticks

⅔ cup yellow or blue cornmeal
⅓ cup all-purpose flour
3 tablespoons sugar
1½ teaspoons baking powder
½ teaspoon LAWRY'S® Seasoned Salt
1 cup milk
2 tablespoons melted butter
1 egg, well beaten
2 tablespoons diced green chiles

In medium bowl, combine cornmeal, flour, sugar, baking powder and Seasoned Salt. In small bowl combine milk, butter and egg; mix well. Add milk mixture to dry ingredients; mix well. Add chiles. Spoon batter into lightly greased corn-shaped molds. Bake in 425°F. oven on lowest rack 20 to 25 minutes. *Makes 12 cornsticks*

Serving Suggestion: Serve warm with whipped honey butter.

Cranberry-Cheese Batter Bread

English-Style Scones

3 eggs
½ cup heavy cream
1½ teaspoons vanilla
2 cups all-purpose flour
2 teaspoons baking powder
¼ teaspoon salt
¼ cup cold butter
¼ cup finely chopped pitted dates
¼ cup golden raisins or currants
1 teaspoon water
6 tablespoons no-sugar-added orange marmalade fruit spread
6 tablespoons softly whipped cream or crème fraîche

1. Preheat oven to 375°F. Beat 2 eggs with cream and vanilla; set aside.

2. Combine flour, baking powder and salt in medium bowl. Cut in butter with pastry blender or 2 knives until mixture resembles coarse crumbs. Stir in dates and raisins. Add egg mixture; mix just until dry ingredients are moistened.

3. With floured hands, knead dough 4 times on lightly floured surface. Place dough on greased cookie sheet; pat into 8-inch circle. With sharp wet knife, gently score dough into 6 wedges, cutting ¾ of the way into dough. Beat remaining egg with water; brush lightly over dough.

4. Bake 18 to 20 minutes or until golden brown. Cool 5 minutes on wire rack. Cut into wedges. Serve warm with marmalade and whipped cream. *Makes 6 scones*

English-Style Scone

Mallomar® Sticky Buns

Preparation Time: 25 minutes
Cook Time: 15 minutes
Total Time: 40 minutes

1 (8-ounce) package refrigerated crescent roll dough
8 MALLOMARS® Chocolate Cakes
Powdered sugar glaze and melted semisweet chocolate, optional

1. Separate crescent roll dough into 8 triangles.

2. Wrap each dough triangle around one cake, pinching seams to seal. Place in 8-inch round cake pan.

3. Bake at 375°F for 15 to 17 minutes or until golden brown. Cool in pan on wire rack for 15 minutes. Remove from pan to serving plate; drizzle with powdered sugar glaze and melted chocolate if desired. Serve warm. *Makes 8 buns*

Fiesta Corn Bread

2 cups all-purpose flour
1½ cups white or yellow cornmeal
1½ cups (6 ounces) shredded mild Cheddar cheese
1 cup (7-ounce can) ORTEGA® Diced Green Chiles
½ cup granulated sugar
1 tablespoon baking powder
1½ teaspoons salt
1½ cups (12 fluid-ounce can) NESTLÉ® CARNATION® Evaporated Milk
½ cup vegetable oil
2 large eggs, lightly beaten

PREHEAT oven to 375°F. Grease 13×9-inch baking pan.

COMBINE flour, cornmeal, cheese, chiles, sugar, baking powder and salt in large bowl. Add evaporated milk, vegetable oil and eggs; stir just until moistened. Spread into prepared baking pan.

BAKE for 30 to 35 minutes or until wooden pick inserted in center comes out clean. Cool in pan on wire rack for 10 minutes; cut into squares. Serve warm.
Makes 24 servings

Upside Down Banana Pecan Muffins

½ cup packed light brown sugar
⅓ cup butter, softened
⅔ cup chopped pecans
2 cups all-purpose flour
½ cup sugar
1 tablespoon baking powder
1 teaspoon ground cinnamon
½ teaspoon salt
2 eggs
½ cup WESSON® Vegetable Oil
2 ripe bananas, mashed
1 teaspoon vanilla extract

In small bowl, combine brown sugar and butter; stir in pecans. Place 1 tablespoon nut mixture into each of 14 greased muffin cups; set aside. In medium bowl, combine flour, sugar, baking powder, cinnamon and salt. In small bowl, beat together eggs, oil, bananas and vanilla. Stir oil mixture into flour mixture just until all ingredients are moistened. Fill prepared muffin cups with batter. Bake at 375°F for 20 minutes or until wooden pick inserted into centers comes out clean. To serve, immediately invert muffins onto plate.

Makes 14 muffins

Greek Spinach-Cheese Rolls

1 loaf (1 pound) frozen bread dough
1 package (10 ounces) frozen chopped spinach, thawed and squeezed dry
¾ cup (3 ounces) crumbled feta cheese
½ cup (2 ounces) shredded reduced-fat Monterey Jack cheese
4 green onions, thinly sliced
1 teaspoon dried dill weed
½ teaspoon garlic powder
½ teaspoon black pepper

1. Thaw bread dough according to package directions. Spray 15 muffin cups with nonstick cooking spray; set aside. Roll out dough on lightly floured surface to 15×9-inch rectangle. (If dough is springy and difficult to roll, cover with plastic wrap and let rest 5 minutes to relax.) Position dough so long edge runs parallel to edge of work surface.

2. Combine spinach, cheeses, green onions, dill weed, garlic powder and pepper in large bowl; mix well.

3. Sprinkle spinach mixture evenly over dough to within 1 inch of long edges. Starting at long edge, roll up snugly, pinching seam closed. Place seam side down; cut roll with serrated knife into 1-inch-wide slices. Place slices cut sides up in prepared muffin cups. Cover with plastic wrap; let stand 30 minutes in warm place until rolls are slightly puffy.

4. Meanwhile, preheat oven to 375°F. Bake 20 to 25 minutes or until golden. Serve warm or at room temperature. Rolls can be stored in refrigerator in airtight container up to 2 days.

Makes 15 rolls

Greek Spinach-Cheese Rolls

Oven-Baked French Toast

12 slices cinnamon bread or cinnamon raisin bread
1 pint (16 ounces) half-and-half or light cream
2 large eggs
6 tablespoons I CAN'T BELIEVE IT'S NOT BUTTER!® Spread, melted
2 tablespoons firmly packed brown sugar
2 teaspoons vanilla extract
1 teaspoon grated orange peel (optional)
¼ teaspoon ground cinnamon
⅛ teaspoon ground nutmeg (optional)

Preheat oven to 350°F.

In lightly greased 13×9-inch baking pan, arrange bread slices in two layers.

In large bowl, with wire whisk, blend remaining ingredients. Evenly pour over bread slices, pressing bread down until some liquid is absorbed and bread does not float. Bake 45 minutes or until center reaches 160°F. and bread is golden brown. Serve hot and sprinkle, if desired, with confectioners' sugar. *Makes 6 servings*

Tip: Freeze leftover French toast in airtight container. To reheat, let French toast come to room temperature, then arrange on baking sheet and bake at 350°F. until hot.

Oven-Baked French Toast

Fire & Ice Brunch Skillet

Prep Time: 5 minutes
Cook Time: 30 minutes

1 (6.8-ounce) package RICE-A-RONI® Spanish Rice
2 tablespoons margarine or butter
1 (16-ounce) jar salsa
⅓ cup sour cream
¼ cup thinly sliced green onions
4 large eggs
1 cup (4 ounces) shredded Cheddar cheese
Chopped cilantro (optional)

1. In large skillet over medium heat, sauté rice-vermicelli mix with margarine until vermicelli is golden brown.

2. Slowly stir in 2 cups water, salsa and Special Seasonings; bring to a boil. Reduce heat to low. Cover; simmer 15 to 20 minutes or until rice is tender.

3. Stir in sour cream and green onions. Using large spoon, make 4 indentations in rice mixture. Break 1 egg into each indentation. Reduce heat to low. Cover; cook 8 minutes or until eggs are cooked to desired doneness.

4. Sprinkle cheese evenly over eggs and rice. Cover; let stand 3 minutes or until cheese is melted. Sprinkle with cilantro, if desired. *Makes 4 servings*

Tip: A twist on Mexican-style huevos rancheros, this dish is perfect for brunch or as a light dinner.

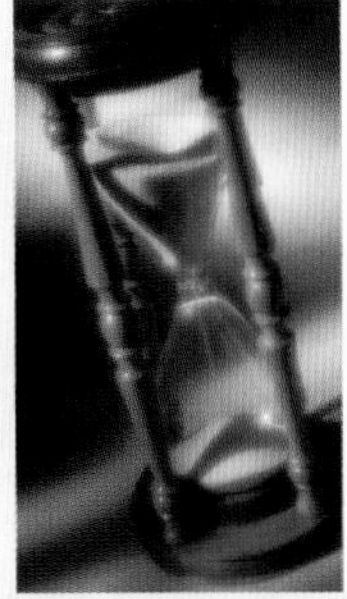

Quick Tip

A poached egg should be cooked until the white is completely set and the yolk is thickened but not hard. Choose very fresh eggs for this recipe to ensure that they will not spread too much when cooked.

Fire & Ice Brunch Skillet

English Muffin Breakfast Sandwiches

2 English muffins, split into halves and toasted
2 tablespoons plain nonfat yogurt
1 tablespoon spicy brown or Dijon mustard
½ teaspoon dried tarragon or basil leaves
4 poached eggs, kept warm
4 large tomato slices (about ¼ inch thick)
4 slices Canadian bacon
2 (1 ounce each) slices reduced-fat Swiss cheese, cut crosswise into halves *or* 1 cup (4 ounces) shredded part-skim mozzarella cheese
Paprika (optional)

1. Preheat broiler.

2. Place muffin halves on baking sheet or broiler pan.

3. Combine yogurt, mustard and tarragon in small bowl and stir until well blended. Spread ¼ of yogurt mixture evenly over each muffin half. Top each muffin half with poached egg, tomato slice and Canadian bacon.

4. Place under broiler about 4 inches from heat source; broil 2 minutes. Top each muffin half with cheese slice half and broil 1 minute or until cheese begins to brown slightly. Sprinkle with paprika, if desired.

Makes 4 servings

Quick Tip

Canadian bacon is more like ham than bacon. This smoked meat is fully cooked so it will heat quickly in dishes like these English Muffin Breakfast Sandwiches. Since Canadian bacon is boneless, there is no waste.

English Muffin Breakfast Sandwich

Ham & Asparagus Brunch Bake

2 boxes UNCLE BEN'S® Long Grain & Wild Rice Original Recipe
1 pound asparagus, cut into 1-inch pieces (about 2½ cups)
2 cups chopped ham
1 cup chopped yellow or red bell pepper
¼ cup finely chopped red onion
1 cup (4 ounces) shredded Swiss cheese

1. In large saucepan, prepare rice mixes according to package directions, adding asparagus during last 5 minutes of cooking.

2. Meanwhile, preheat oven to 350°F. Grease 11×7½-inch baking dish.

3. Remove rice mixture from heat. Add ham, bell pepper and onion; mix well. Place mixture in prepared baking dish; sprinkle with cheese.

4. Bake 25 to 30 minutes or until mixture is heated through. *Makes 8 servings*

Variation: Substitute UNCLE BEN'S® Brand Butter & Herb Long Grain & Wild Rice for the Original Recipe Long Grain & Wild Rice.

Tip: This dish can be prepared ahead of time through step 3. Cover with foil and refrigerate several hours or overnight. Bake, covered, in preheated 350°F oven for 15 minutes. Remove foil and continue to bake until heated through, about 10 minutes.

Quick Tip

After rinsing fresh asparagus, snap off and discard the fibrous portion of the stalks. If the stalks are thick, peeling them with a vegetable peeler will result in quicker cooking.

Ham & Asparagus Brunch Bake

Puff Pancake with Summer Berries

Summer Berries (recipe follows)
4 tablespoons butter or margarine, divided
2 eggs
½ cup all-purpose flour
½ cup milk
1 tablespoon sugar
¼ teaspoon salt

1. Prepare Summer Berries; set aside. Preheat oven to 425°F. Place 2 tablespoons butter in ovenproof skillet. Place skillet in oven 3 minutes or until butter is bubbly. Swirl pan to coat bottom and side.

2. Beat eggs in medium bowl with electric mixer at high speed. Add flour, milk, remaining 2 tablespoons butter, sugar and salt; beat until smooth.

3. Pour batter into prepared skillet. Bake 15 minutes.

4. *Reduce oven temperature to 350°F.* Continue baking 10 to 15 minutes or until pancake is puffed and golden brown.

5. Serve pancake in skillet with Summer Berries.

Makes 6 servings

Summer Berries

2 cups blueberries
1 cup sliced strawberries
1 cup raspberries
Sugar to taste
Whipping cream (optional)

Combine blueberries, strawberries and raspberries in medium bowl. Gently toss with sugar. Let stand 5 minutes. Top with whipping cream, if desired.

Puff Pancake with Summer Berries

Apple Brunch Strata

- ½ pound sausage, casing removed
- 4 cups cubed French bread
- 2 cups diced peeled Michigan Apples
- ¼ cup sliced green onions
- ⅓ cup sliced black olives
- 1½ cups (6 ounces) shredded sharp Cheddar cheese
- 2 cups reduced-fat milk
- 8 eggs
- 2 teaspoons spicy brown mustard
- ½ teaspoon salt
- ¼ teaspoon black pepper
- Paprika

1. Brown sausage in skillet over medium-high heat. Drain on paper towels; set aside.

2. Spray 13×9×2-inch baking dish with nonstick cooking spray. Layer half of bread cubes in bottom of dish. Crumble sausage over bread. Top with Michigan Apples, green onions, olives and cheese. Place remaining bread on top.

3. Mix milk, eggs, mustard, salt and pepper in medium bowl; pour over bread. Cover with foil and refrigerate 4 hours or overnight.

4. Preheat oven to 350°F. Bake, covered, 45 minutes. Remove foil and bake 15 minutes or until center is set. Let stand 15 minutes before serving. Sprinkle with paprika, if desired.

Makes 8 servings

Tip: Suggested Michigan Apple varieties to use include Empire, Gala, Golden Delicious, Ida Red, Jonagold, Jonathan, McIntosh or Rome.

Variation: Substitute 1 can (20 ounces) sliced Michigan Apples, drained and chopped for fresh Apples.

Favorite recipe from *Michigan Apple Committee*

Apple Brunch Strata

Eggs Rancheros

Ranchero Sauce

1 can (16 ounces) whole tomatoes, undrained and chopped
1 can (4 ounces) chopped green chilies, drained
½ cup chopped onion
1 tablespoon white wine vinegar
¼ teaspoon salt

Eggs

1 tablespoon vegetable oil
4 eggs
Salt and pepper to taste
1 can (30 ounces) refried beans
1 cup (4 ounces) shredded Cheddar cheese
4 corn tortillas

1. For Ranchero Sauce, combine tomatoes, chilies, onion, vinegar and salt in medium saucepan. Cook, stirring occasionally, over medium heat until onion is tender, about 20 minutes. Keep warm.

2. For eggs, heat oil in large skillet over medium-low heat. Break eggs into skillet. Season with salt and pepper. Cook 2 to 3 minutes or until eggs are set. Turn eggs for over-easy eggs.

3. Heat beans in medium saucepan. Spoon beans onto 4 warmed plates; sprinkle evenly with cheese.

4. Heat tortillas. Place 1 tortilla on each plate beside beans; top each tortilla with 1 egg. Spoon warm Ranchero Sauce over eggs.

Makes 4 servings

TIP: To heat tortillas in a conventional oven, wrap in foil and place in 350°F oven about 10 minutes. To heat tortillas in a microwave oven, wrap loosely in a damp paper towel. Heat at HIGH (100%) about 1 minute.

Cooking Eggs: When cooking eggs, remember that too high a temperature will cause them to be tough and rubbery. Use either low or medium heat.

Egg Rancheros

Biscuits 'n Gravy

Biscuits

- WESSON® No-Stick Cooking Spray
- 2 cups self-rising flour
- 2 teaspoons sugar
- 1½ teaspoons baking powder
- ¾ cup buttermilk
- ¼ cup WESSON® Vegetable Oil

Gravy

- 1 pound bulk pork sausage
- ¼ cup all-purpose flour
- 2 cups milk
- ¼ teaspoon salt
- ¼ teaspoon pepper

Biscuits

Preheat oven to 450°F. Lightly spray a baking sheet with Wesson® Cooking Spray. In a large bowl, combine flour, sugar and baking powder; blend well. In a small bowl, whisk together buttermilk and Wesson® Oil; add to dry ingredients and mix until dough is moist but not sticky. On a lightly floured surface, knead dough lightly 4 or 5 times. Roll dough to a ¾-inch thickness; cut with a 4-inch biscuit cutter. Knead any scraps together and repeat cutting method. Place biscuits on baking sheet and bake 10 to 15 minutes or until lightly browned. Keep warm.

Gravy

Meanwhile, in a large skillet, cook and crumble sausage until brown. Reserve ¼ cup of drippings in skillet; drain sausage well. Set aside. Add flour to drippings in skillet; stir until smooth. Cook over medium heat for 2 to 3 minutes or until dark brown, stirring constantly. Gradually add milk, stirring constantly until smooth and thickened. (Use more milk if necessary to achieve desired consistency.) Stir in salt, pepper and sausage; heat through. Serve over hot split biscuits.

Makes 6 servings (2 biscuits each)

Stuffed French Toast

1 (8-ounce) package cream cheese, softened
2 tablespoons sugar
1½ teaspoons vanilla, divided
¼ teaspoon ground cinnamon
½ cup chopped walnuts or pecans
1 (1-pound) loaf French bread
4 eggs
1 cup whipping cream or half-and-half
½ teaspoon nutmeg
1 cup (12-ounce jar) SMUCKER'S® Apricot Preserves
½ cup orange juice
½ teaspoon almond extract
Fresh fruit

Beat together cream cheese, sugar, 1 teaspoon vanilla and cinnamon until fluffy. Stir in nuts; set aside.

Cut bread into 10 to 12 (1½-inch) slices; cut pocket in top of each slice. Fill each pocket with about 1½ tablespoons cream cheese mixture.

Beat together eggs, whipping cream, remaining ½ teaspoon vanilla and nutmeg. Using tongs, dip bread slices in egg mixture, being careful not to squeeze out filling. Cook on a lightly greased griddle until both sides are golden brown. (To keep cooked slices hot for serving, place on baking sheet in warm oven.)

Meanwhile, combine and heat preserves and orange juice. Stir in almond extract. To serve, drizzle apricot mixture over French toast. Serve with fresh fruit.

Makes 10 to 12 slices

Honey Roasted Ham Biscuits

1 (10-ounce) can refrigerated buttermilk biscuits
2 cups (12 ounces) diced CURE 81® ham
½ cup honey mustard
¼ cup finely chopped honey roasted peanuts, divided

Heat oven to 400°F. Separate biscuits. Place in muffin pans, pressing gently into bottom and up sides of pan. In bowl, combine ham, honey mustard and 2 tablespoons peanuts. Spoon ham mixture evenly into biscuit cups. Sprinkle with remaining 2 tablespoons peanuts. Bake 15 to 17 minutes. *Makes 10 servings*

Hearty Spam™ Breakfast Skillet

2 cups frozen diced or shredded potatoes, thawed
½ cup chopped onion
¼ medium green bell pepper, cut into 1-inch thin strips
¼ medium red or yellow bell pepper, cut into 1-inch thin strips
2 teaspoons vegetable oil
1 (12-ounce) can SPAM® Luncheon Meat, cut into julienne strips
1 (8-ounce) carton frozen fat-free egg product, thawed *or* 4 eggs
¼ teaspoon dried basil leaves
⅛ teaspoon salt
⅛ teaspoon black pepper
6 drops hot pepper sauce
¼ cup (1 ounce) shredded Cheddar cheese

In large nonstick skillet over medium-high heat, cook potatoes, onion and bell peppers in oil 5 minutes, stirring constantly. Add SPAM®; cook and stir 5 minutes. In small bowl, combine egg product, basil, salt, black pepper and hot pepper sauce; blend well. Pour over mixture in skillet. Cover. Cook over medium-low heat 8 to 12 minutes or until set. Sprinkle with cheese; remove from heat. *Makes 6 servings*

Honey Roasted Ham Biscuits

Pizza for Breakfast

1 (6½-ounce) package pizza crust mix
1 pound BOB EVANS® Original Recipe Roll Sausage
1 cup diced fresh or drained canned tomatoes
8 ounces fresh mushrooms, sliced
1½ cups (6 ounces) shredded mozzarella cheese, divided
1½ cups (6 ounces) shredded sharp Cheddar cheese, divided
4 eggs
Salt and pepper to taste
Salsa (optional)

Preheat oven to 350°F. Prepare crust mix according to package directions. Spread pizza dough into greased 13×9-inch baking dish, making sure dough evenly covers bottom and 2 inches up sides of dish. Crumble and cook sausage in medium skillet until browned; drain well on paper towels. Top crust with sausage, tomatoes, mushrooms, 1 cup mozzarella cheese and 1 cup Cheddar cheese. Bake 8 to 10 minutes or until crust is golden brown at edges. Remove from oven. Whisk eggs, salt and pepper in small bowl; pour over pizza. Return to oven; bake 7 to 9 minutes more or until eggs are set. Immediately sprinkle with remaining cheeses. Serve hot with salsa, if desired. Refrigerate leftovers. *Makes 8 to 10 servings*

Note: Refrigerated crescent roll dough may be used instead of pizza crust mix. Seal edges together and stretch to fit baking dish.

Pizza for Breakfast

Monte Cristo Sandwiches

2 tablespoons honey mustard, divided
12 thin slices white or egg bread, divided
4 ounces sliced deli turkey breast
8 thin slices (4 ounces) Swiss cheese, divided
4 ounces smoked sliced deli ham, divided
2 eggs, beaten
¼ cup milk
Dash ground nutmeg
2 to 3 tablespoons butter or margarine
Powdered sugar
Strawberry or raspberry preserves

1. Preheat oven to 450°F.

2. To assemble one 3-decker sandwich, spread ½ teaspoon mustard over 1 side of each of 3 bread slices. Place ¼ of turkey and 1 cheese slice over mustard on 1 bread slice. Top with second bread slice, mustard side up.

3. Place ¼ of ham and 1 cheese slice on top of bread. Top with remaining bread slice, mustard side down, pressing gently together. Repeat with remaining mustard, bread, turkey, cheese and ham to make 4 sandwiches.

4. Combine eggs, milk and nutmeg in shallow dish or pie plate.

5. Melt 1 tablespoon butter in large nonstick skillet over medium heat. Dip both sides of each sandwich briefly in egg mixture, letting excess drip back into dish.

6. Fry 1 sandwich at a time in skillet 4 minutes or until browned, turning halfway through cooking. Transfer sandwiches to greased or foil-lined baking sheet. Repeat with remaining sandwiches, adding butter to skillet as needed.

7. Bake sandwiches 5 to 7 minutes or until heated through and cheese is melted. Cut each sandwich in half diagonally; sprinkle lightly with powdered sugar. Serve immediately with preserves.

Makes 4 servings

Monte Cristo Sandwich

Sunrise Pancakes

Vanilla Cream Syrup (recipe follows)
1 cup all-purpose flour
2 tablespoons sugar
1 teaspoon baking powder
½ teaspoon baking soda
½ teaspoon salt
2 eggs, slightly beaten
½ cup plain yogurt
½ cup water
2½ to 3 tablespoons butter or margarine, melted and divided

1. Prepare Vanilla Cream Syrup; set aside.

2. Combine flour, sugar, baking powder, baking soda and salt in large bowl. Combine eggs, yogurt and water in medium bowl. Whisk in 2 tablespoons butter. Pour liquid ingredients into dry ingredients all at once; stir just until moistened.

3. Heat griddle or large skillet over medium heat; brush with ½ tablespoon butter. For each pancake, pour about ¼ cup batter onto hot griddle; spread batter out to make 5-inch circle. Cook until tops of pancakes are bubbly and appear dry; turn and cook about 2 minutes or until browned. (Brush griddle with additional butter, if needed, to prevent sticking.) Serve pancakes with Vanilla Cream Syrup.

Makes about 8 pancakes

Hint: Overmixing pancake batter produces tough pancakes. Mix the batter only until the dry ingredients are moistened. The batter may still be lumpy.

Vanilla Cream Syrup

½ cup sugar
½ cup light corn syrup
½ cup whipping cream
1 fresh nectarine, chopped
1 teaspoon vanilla extract

Combine sugar, corn syrup and cream in 1-quart saucepan. Cook over medium heat until sugar is dissolved, stirring constantly. Simmer 2 minutes or until syrup thickens slightly. Remove from heat. Stir in nectarine and vanilla. *Makes 1 cup*

Sunrise Pancakes

Egg and Sausage Breakfast Strudel

1 pound BOB EVANS® Original Recipe Roll Sausage
¾ cup finely grated Parmesan cheese
1 (10¾-ounce) can condensed cream of mushroom soup
2 hard-cooked eggs, cut into ¼-inch cubes
½ cup thinly sliced green onions
¼ cup chopped fresh parsley
1 (16-ounce) package frozen phyllo dough, thawed according to package directions
Butter-flavored nonstick cooking spray *or* ½ cup melted butter or margarine

Crumble and cook sausage in medium skillet until browned. Drain off any drippings; place in medium bowl. Add cheese, soup, eggs, green onions and parsley; stir gently until blended. Cover and chill at least 4 hours.

Preheat oven to 375°F. Layer 4 sheets of phyllo dough, coating each sheet with cooking spray or brushing with melted butter before stacking. Cut stack in half lengthwise. Shape ⅓ cup filling into log and place at bottom end of 1 stack. Fold in sides to cover filling; roll up phyllo dough and filling jelly roll style. Seal edges and spray roll with cooking spray or brush with butter. Repeat with remaining phyllo dough and filling. Place rolls on ungreased baking sheet, seam sides down. Bake 15 to 20 minutes or until golden brown. Serve hot. Refrigerate leftovers.

Makes 10 strudels

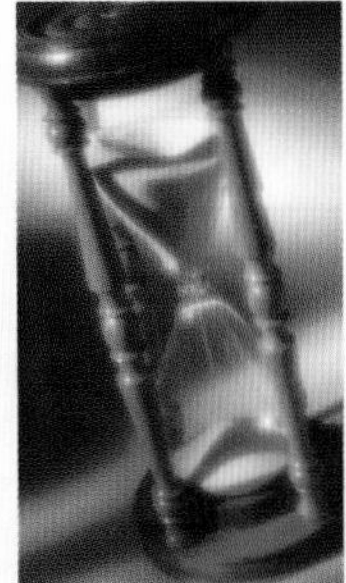

Quick Tip

Unbaked strudels can be wrapped and refrigerated up to 24 hours before baking. Or, they may be wrapped and frozen for up to 1 month. For frozen strudel, allow additional baking time.

Egg and Sausage Breakfast Strudel

Ham & Cheddar Frittata

3 eggs
3 egg whites
½ teaspoon salt
½ teaspoon freshly ground black pepper
1½ cups (4 ounces) frozen broccoli florets, thawed
6 ounces deli smoked ham, cut into ½-inch cubes (1¼ cups)
⅓ cup drained bottled roasted red bell peppers, cut into thin strips
1 tablespoon butter
½ cup (2 ounces) shredded sharp Cheddar cheese

1. Preheat broiler with rack about 5 inches from heat source.

2. Beat eggs, egg whites, salt and pepper in large bowl until blended. Stir in broccoli, ham and pepper strips.

3. Melt butter over medium heat in 10-inch ovenproof skillet with sloping sides. Pour egg mixture into skillet; cover. Cook 5 to 6 minutes or until eggs are set around edges. (Center will be wet.)

4. Sprinkle cheese over frittata. Transfer skillet to broiler; broil 2 minutes or until eggs are set in center. Let stand 5 minutes; cut into wedges. Makes 4 servings

Fluffy Scrambled Eggs with Fresh Herbs

6 large eggs
¼ cup milk, half-and-half or light cream
¼ teaspoon salt
⅛ teaspoon ground white pepper
2 tablespoons I CAN'T BELIEVE IT'S NOT BUTTER!® Spread
⅓ cup finely chopped onion or shallots
1 teaspoon finely chopped fresh tarragon, parsley, chive, basil, marjoram or oregano leaves

In medium bowl, with wire whisk, blend eggs, milk, salt and pepper.

In 12-inch nonstick skillet, melt I Can't Believe It's Not Butter! Spread over medium-high heat and cook onion, stirring occasionally, 3 minutes or until onion is tender. Reduce heat to medium and stir in egg mixture until eggs and onions are combined. Stir in herbs and cook, stirring frequently, until eggs are set. *Makes 2 servings*

Ham & Cheddar Frittata

Steak Hash

2 tablespoons vegetable oil
1 green bell pepper, chopped
½ medium onion, chopped
1 pound russet potatoes, baked, peeled and chopped
8 ounces cooked steak or roast beef, cut into 1-inch cubes
Salt and black pepper
¼ cup (1 ounce) shredded Monterey Jack cheese
4 eggs

1. Heat oil in medium skillet over medium heat. Add bell pepper and onion; cook until tender. Stir in potatoes; reduce heat to low. Cover and cook, stirring occasionally, about 10 minutes or until potatoes are hot.

2. Stir in steak; season with salt and pepper. Sprinkle with cheese. Cover; cook about 5 minutes or until steak is hot and cheese is melted. Spoon onto 4 plates.

3. Prepare eggs as desired; top each serving with 1 egg. *Makes 4 servings*

Hawaiian Breakfast Wrap

Prep Time: 15 minutes

6 eggs
¼ cup milk or water
¼ cup chopped ham
¼ cup chopped DOLE® Red or Green Bell Pepper
2 tablespoons margarine
1 can (8 ounces) DOLE® Crushed Pineapple, drained
4 (8-inch) flour tortillas

• Beat together eggs and milk in medium bowl until blended. Set aside.

• Cook ham and bell pepper in hot margarine over medium heat in large skillet until ham is lightly browned and vegetables are tender-crisp. Stir in egg mixture and crushed pineapple. Scramble until desired doneness, stirring constantly.

• Evenly divide egg mixture onto flour tortillas. Roll sides up. Serve with watermelon wedges and lime slice, if desired. Serve immediately. *Makes 4 servings*

Steak Hash

Egg & Sausage Casserole

- ½ pound pork sausage
- 3 tablespoons margarine or butter, divided
- 2 tablespoons all-purpose flour
- ¼ teaspoon salt
- ¼ teaspoon black pepper
- 1¼ cups milk
- 2 cups frozen hash brown potatoes
- 4 eggs, hard-cooked and sliced
- ½ cup cornflake crumbs
- ¼ cup sliced green onions

1. Preheat oven to 350°F. Spray 2-quart oval baking dish with nonstick cooking spray.

2. Crumble sausage into large skillet; brown over medium-high heat until no longer pink, stirring to separate meat. Drain sausage on paper towels. Discard fat and wipe skillet with paper towel.

3. Melt 2 tablespoons margarine in same skillet over medium heat. Stir in flour, salt and pepper until smooth. Gradually stir in milk; cook and stir until thickened. Add sausage, potatoes and eggs; stir to combine. Pour into prepared dish.

4. Melt remaining 1 tablespoon margarine. Combine cornflake crumbs and melted margarine in small bowl; sprinkle evenly over casserole.

5. Bake, uncovered, 30 minutes or until hot and bubbly. Sprinkle with onions.

Makes 6 servings

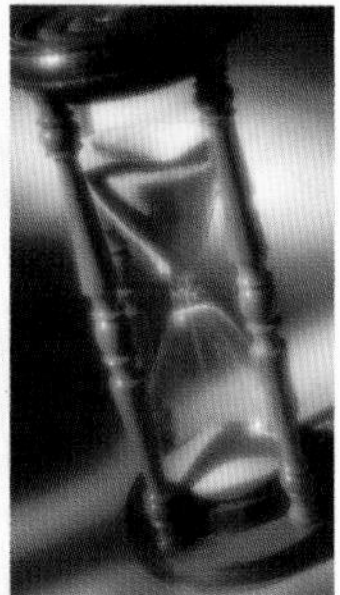

Quick Tip

To hard-cook eggs, place them in a saucepan and cover with cold water. Bring water to a boil; cover pan and remove from heat. Let stand 15 minutes; pour off water. Cover eggs with ice water until cool.

Egg & Sausage Casserole

Waffles

2¼ cups all-purpose flour
2 tablespoons sugar
1 tablespoon baking powder
½ teaspoon salt
2 cups milk
2 eggs, beaten
¼ cup vegetable oil

1. Preheat waffle iron; grease lightly.

2. Sift flour, sugar, baking powder and salt in large bowl. Combine milk, eggs and oil in medium bowl. Stir liquid ingredients into dry ingredients until moistened.

3. For each waffle, pour about ¾ cup batter onto waffle iron. Close and bake until steaming stops.* Garnish as desired. *Makes about 6 round waffles*

**Check the manufacturer's directions for recommended amount of batter and baking time.*

Chocolate Waffles: Substitute ¼ cup unsweetened cocoa powder for ¼ cup flour and add ¼ teaspoon vanilla to liquid ingredients. Proceed as directed above.

Tip: For crispier waffles, use less batter and let them cook for a few seconds longer after the steaming has stopped.

Huevos Rancheros Tostados

1 can (8 ounces) tomato sauce
⅓ cup prepared salsa or picante sauce
¼ cup chopped fresh cilantro or thinly sliced green onions
4 large eggs
Butter or margarine
4 (6-inch) corn tortillas, crisply fried or 4 prepared tostada shells
1 cup (4 ounces) SARGENTO® Taco Blend Shredded Cheese

Combine tomato sauce, salsa and cilantro; heat in microwave oven or in saucepan over medium-high heat until hot. Fry eggs in butter, sunny side up. Place one egg on each tortilla; top with sauce. Sprinkle with cheese. *Makes 4 servings*

Variation: Spread tortillas with heated refried beans before topping with eggs, if desired.

Waffle

Ham and Cheese Bread Pudding

1 small loaf (8 ounces) sourdough, country French or Italian bread, cut into 1-inch-thick slices
3 tablespoons butter or margarine, softened
8 ounces ham or smoked ham, cubed
2 cups (8 ounces) shredded mild or sharp Cheddar cheese
3 eggs
2 cups milk
1 teaspoon dry mustard
½ teaspoon salt
⅛ teaspoon white pepper

1. Grease 11×7-inch baking dish. Spread 1 side of each bread slice with butter. Cut into 1-inch cubes; place on bottom of prepared dish. Top with ham; sprinkle with cheese.

2. Beat eggs in medium bowl. Whisk in milk, mustard, salt and pepper. Pour egg mixture evenly over bread mixture. Cover; refrigerate at least 6 hours or overnight.

3. Preheat oven to 350°F.

4. Bake bread pudding uncovered 45 to 50 minutes or until puffed and golden brown and knife inserted in center comes out clean. Garnish, if desired. Cut into squares. Serve immediately. *Makes 8 servings*

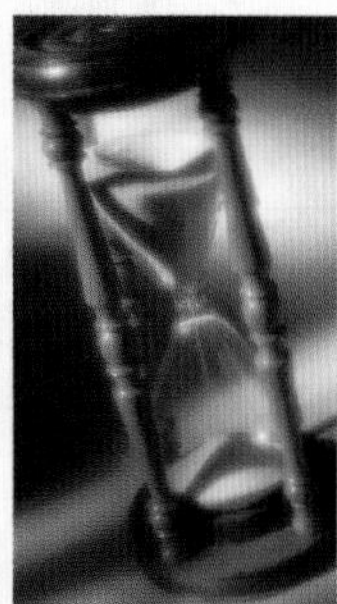

Quick Tip

When leftover ham is not available for Ham and Cheese Bread Pudding, purchase a 1-inch-thick slice of ham at the supermarket deli counter. You will need about 1½ cups of ham cubes for this recipe.

Ham and Cheese Bread Pudding

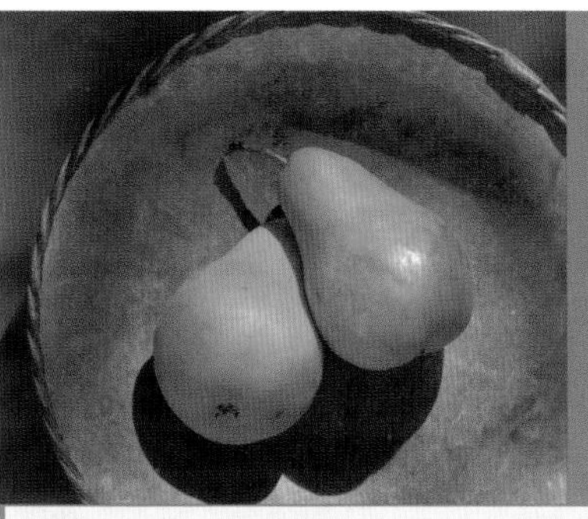

Decadent Triple Layer Mud Pie

Prep Time: 10 minutes
Chilling Time: 3 hours

- **¼ cup sweetened condensed milk**
- **2 (1-ounce) squares semi-sweet baking chocolate, melted**
- **1 (6-ounce) READY CRUST® Chocolate Pie Crust**
- **¾ cup chopped pecans, toasted**
- **2 cups cold milk**
- **2 (4-serving-size) packages JELL-O® Chocolate Flavor Instant Pudding & Pie Filling**
- **1 (8-ounce) tub COOL WHIP® Whipped Topping, thawed, divided**

1. Combine sweetened condensed milk and chocolate in medium bowl; stir until smooth. Pour into crust. Press nuts evenly onto chocolate mixture in crust. Refrigerate 10 minutes.

2. Pour milk into large bowl. Add pudding mixes. Beat with wire whisk 2 minutes or until smooth. (Mixture will be thick.) Spread 1½ cups pudding over chocolate mixture in crust. Immediately stir half of whipped topping into remaining pudding. Spread over pudding in crust. Top with remaining whipped topping.

3. Refrigerate 3 hours or until set. Garnish as desired. Refrigerate leftovers.

Makes 8 servings

Decadent Triple Layer Mud Pie

Fluffy Lemon Berry Pie

Prep Time: 10 minutes
Chilling Time: 3 hours

4 ounces cream cheese, softened
1½ cups cold milk
2 (4-serving size) packages JELL-O® Lemon Flavor Instant Pudding & Pie Filling
1 (8-ounce) tub COOL WHIP® Whipped Topping, thawed
1 (6-ounce) READY CRUST® Shortbread or Graham Cracker Pie Crust
1 cup blueberries, raspberries or sliced strawberries

1. Beat cream cheese in large bowl with wire whisk until smooth. Gradually beat in milk until well blended. Add pudding mixes. Beat 2 minutes or until smooth. Immediately stir in half of whipped topping.

2. Spoon into crust. Top with remaining whipped topping.

3. Refrigerate 3 hours or until set. Garnish with berries. Refrigerate leftovers.

Makes 8 servings

Planters® Perfect Pecan Pie

3 eggs
1 cup light corn syrup
1 cup sugar
2 tablespoons margarine or butter, melted
1 teaspoon vanilla extract
⅛ teaspoon salt
1 cup PLANTERS® Pecan Halves
1 (9-inch) unbaked pastry shell
COOL WHIP® Whipped Topping and PLANTERS® Pecan Halves, for garnish

1. Beat eggs slightly. Stir in corn syrup, sugar, margarine or butter, vanilla and salt until blended. Stir in pecan halves; pour into pastry shell.

2. Bake at 400°F for 15 minutes. *Reduce temperature to 350°F*, bake for 25 to 30 minutes more or until lightly browned and completely puffed across top. Cool completely.

3. Serve with whipped topping and pecan halves if desired.

Makes 8 servings

Fluffy Lemon Berry Pie

Mocha Decadence Pie

4 squares (1 ounce each) semisweet chocolate
2 cups heavy cream, divided
½ cup plus 1 tablespoon sugar, divided
3 eggs
2 teaspoons instant coffee granules
1 teaspoon vanilla, divided
1 packaged graham cracker crust (6 ounces)

Place chocolate in small microwavable dish. Microwave at HIGH 1½ minutes or until melted, stirring after 1 minute. Set aside.

Combine 1 cup heavy cream and ½ cup sugar in medium saucepan over medium heat. Cook until sugar is melted, stirring constantly. Beat eggs in small bowl. Stir ¼ cup cream mixture into eggs. Stir egg mixture back into cream mixture. Stir constantly 4 to 5 minutes or until thickened. Pour into large bowl. Beat in melted chocolate, coffee granules and ½ teaspoon vanilla on low speed of electric mixer. Increase speed to medium. Beat 2 minutes. Pour into pie shell. Cool 15 minutes. Cover and refrigerate 3 hours or overnight.

Beat remaining 1 cup cream in medium bowl with electric mixer on high speed 1 minute. Add remaining 1 tablespoon sugar and remaining ½ teaspoon vanilla. Beat until mixture forms soft peaks. Top each slice with whipped cream.

Makes 8 servings

Quick Tip

Heavy cream is often referred to as whipping cream. For the best results when whipping cream, the cream, the bowl and beaters should be cold. This will increase the volume of the whipped cream.

Mocha Decadence Pie

Pecan "Brickle" Apple Pie

Crust

1 (9-inch) Classic CRISCO® Double Crust (recipe page 286)

Filling

¼ cup butter or margarine, melted
½ cup loosely packed light brown sugar, divided
1 cup chopped pecans, divided
¾ cup almond brickle chips, divided
6 cups sliced peeled Granny Smith, Jonathan or Rome Beauty apples (about 2 pounds or 6 medium apples)
½ cup granulated sugar
2 tablespoons all-purpose flour
1 tablespoon fresh lemon juice
¾ teaspoon ground cinnamon
¼ teaspoon ground nutmeg
⅛ teaspoon salt
⅛ teaspoon ground ginger
3 tablespoons butter or margarine, cut into pieces

Glaze

Milk
Granulated sugar

1. Prepare 9-inch double crust dough as directed through first 3 steps only. Divide dough in half. Roll and press bottom crust into 9- or 9½-inch deep-dish Pyrex® pie plate, reserving pastry scraps. *Do not bake.* Heat oven to 425°F.

2. For filling, pour melted butter into unbaked pie crust. Sprinkle with ¼ cup brown sugar, ⅓ cup chopped nuts and ¼ cup brickle chips.

3. Place apples in large bowl. Combine ½ cup granulated sugar, remaining ¼ cup brown sugar, flour, lemon juice, cinnamon, nutmeg, salt and ginger in small bowl. Sprinkle over apples. Toss to coat. Spoon one third of apple mixture over brickle chips. Sprinkle with ⅓ cup nuts and ¼ cup chips. Cover with one-third of apple mixture. Sprinkle with remaining ⅓ cup nuts and ¼ cup chips. Cover with remaining apple mixture. Dot with butter. Moisten pastry edge with water.

4. Roll top crust same as bottom. Cut apple and leaf shapes into top crust. Remove and place on baking sheet.

continued on page 286

Pecan "Brickle" Apple Pie

Pecan "Brickle" Apple Pie, continued

5. Bake shapes at 425°F for 8 minutes or until golden brown. *Do not overbake.*

6. Lift top crust onto filled pie. Trim ½ inch beyond edge of pie plate. Fold top edge under bottom crust. Flute.

7. For glaze, brush top crust with milk. Sprinkle with granulated sugar.

8. Place pie in oven. *Reduce oven temperature to 350°F.* Bake 1 hour 30 minutes or until apples are tender and crust is golden brown. *Do not overbake.* Place separately baked apple and leaf cutouts into areas from which they were cut. Cool to room temperature before serving. *Makes one 9- or 9½-inch deep-dish pie (8 servings)*

Classic Crisco® Double Crust

2 cups all-purpose flour
1 teaspoon salt
¾ CRISCO® Stick or ¾ cup CRISCO® all-vegetable shortening
5 tablespoons cold water (or more as needed)

1. Spoon flour into measuring cup and level. Combine flour and salt in medium bowl.

2. Cut in ¾ cup shortening using pastry blender or 2 knives until all flour is blended to form pea-size chunks.

3. Sprinkle with water, 1 tablespoon at a time. Toss lightly with fork until dough forms a ball.

4. Press dough between hands to form 5- to 6-inch "pancake." Flour rolling surface and rolling pin lightly. Roll both halves of dough into circle. Trim one circle of dough 1 inch larger than upside-down pie plate. Carefully remove trimmed dough. Set aside to reroll and use for pastry cutout garnish, if desired.

5. Fold dough into quarters. Unfold and press into pie plate. Trim edge even with plate. Add desired filling to unbaked crust. Moisten pastry edge with water. Lift top crust onto filled pie. Trim ½ inch beyond edge of pie plate. Fold top edge under bottom crust. Flute. Cut slits in top crust to allow steam to escape. Follow baking directions given for that recipe. *Makes 1 (9-inch) double crust*

Super Luscious Oreo® Cheesecake Pie

Prep Time: 10 minutes plus refrigerating

4 ounces PHILADELPHIA® Cream Cheese, softened
2 cups cold milk, divided
2 packages (4-serving size each) JELL-O® Pistachio Flavor Instant Pudding & Pie Filling
1 tub (8 ounces) COOL WHIP® Whipped Topping, thawed
1 package (8 ounces) Mini OREO® Chocolate Sandwich Cookies, divided
1 OREO® Pie Crust (9 inch)

BEAT cream cheese and ½ cup milk in large bowl with wire whisk until smooth. Add remaining 1½ cups milk and pudding mixes. Beat with wire whisk 2 minutes or until well blended. Stir in whipped topping until smooth and well blended. Reserving 20 cookies, gently stir remaining cookies into pudding mixture. Spoon into crust.

REFRIGERATE 4 hours or until set. Garnish by placing remaining cookies around edge of pie.

Makes 8 servings

Helpful Hint: Soften cream cheese in microwave on HIGH 15 seconds.

Great Substitute: Prepare cheesecake as directed above, substituting 20 chopped or broken OREO® Chocolate Sandwich Cookies for the Mini OREO® Chocolate Sandwich Cookies, and stirring all cookies into the filling. Garnish as desired.

CHIPS AHOY!® Pistachio Cheesecake: Prepare cheesecake as directed above, substituting NILLA® Pie Crust for the OREO® Pie Crust and 20 chopped or broken CHIPS AHOY!® Chocolate Chip Cookies for the Mini OREO® Chocolate Sandwich Cookies, and stirring all cookies into the filling. Garnish as desired.

Upside-Down Hot Fudge Sundae Pie

⅔ cup butter or margarine
⅓ cup HERSHEY'S® Cocoa
2 eggs
¼ cup milk
1 teaspoon vanilla extract
1 cup packed light brown sugar
½ cup granulated sugar
1 tablespoon all-purpose flour
⅛ teaspoon salt
1 unbaked 9-inch pie crust
2 bananas, peeled and thinly sliced
Ice cream, any flavor
Whipped topping

1. Heat oven to 350°F.

2. Melt butter in medium saucepan over low heat. Add cocoa; stir until smooth. Remove from heat. Stir together eggs, milk and vanilla in small bowl. Add egg mixture to cocoa mixture; stir with whisk until smooth and slightly thickened. Add brown sugar, granulated sugar, flour and salt; stir with whisk until smooth. Pour mixture into unbaked crust.

3. Bake 30 to 35 minutes until edge is set. (Center will be soft.) Cool about 2 hours. Just before serving, top each serving with banana slices, ice cream and whipped topping. *Makes 8 servings*

Upside-Down Hot Fudge Sundae Pie

Lemon Dream Pie

1 prepared or homemade 9-inch pie shell
1½ cups water
1 cup honey
½ cup lemon juice
⅓ cup cornstarch
2 tablespoons butter or margarine
1 teaspoon grated lemon peel
¼ teaspoon salt
4 egg yolks, lightly beaten
1½ cups heavy whipping cream, whipped to soft peaks

Bake empty pie shell according to package directions until golden brown. In medium saucepan, combine water, honey, lemon juice, cornstarch, butter, lemon peel and salt. Bring to a boil, stirring constantly. Boil for 5 minutes. Remove from heat. Stir small amount into yolks. Pour yolk mixture back into honey mixture; mix thoroughly. Pour into pie shell. Chill. To serve, top with whipped cream. *Makes 8 servings*

Favorite recipe from *National Honey Board*

Decadent Chocolate Cream Pie

Prep Time: 10 minutes plus refrigerating

2 packages (4-serving size each) JELL-O® Chocolate Flavor Cook & Serve Pudding & Pie Filling (not Instant)
3½ cups half-and-half
1 baked pastry shell (9 inch), cooled
1 tub (8 ounces) COOL WHIP® Whipped Topping, thawed

STIR pudding mixes and half-and-half in medium saucepan with wire whisk until blended. Stirring constantly, cook over medium heat until mixture comes to full boil. Pour into pastry shell.

REFRIGERATE 3 hours or until set. Garnish pie with whipped topping.
Makes 8 servings

Great Substitute: Use an OREO Pie Crust (9 inch) instead of a pastry shell. Garnish pie with chocolate shavings or chocolate sprinkles.

Lemon Dream Pie

Black & White Brownie Bottom Pudding Pie

Prep Time: 15 minutes
Bake Time: 25 minutes

4 squares BAKER'S® Semi-Sweet Baking Chocolate
1/4 cup (1/2 stick) butter or margarine
3/4 cup sugar
2 eggs
1 teaspoon vanilla
1/2 cup flour
2 1/2 cups cold milk
2 packages (4-serving size each) JELL-O® White Chocolate or Vanilla Flavor Instant Pudding & Pie Filling

HEAT oven to 350°F (325°F for glass pie plate).

MICROWAVE chocolate and butter in small microwavable bowl on HIGH 2 minutes or until butter is melted. Stir until chocolate is completely melted.

STIR in sugar, eggs and vanilla. Blend in flour. Spread batter in greased 9-inch pie plate. Bake 25 minutes or until toothpick inserted in center comes out with fudgy crumbs. *Do not overbake.* Lightly press center with bottom of measuring cup or back of spoon to form slight depression. Cool on wire rack.

POUR milk into large bowl. Add pudding mixes. Beat with wire whisk 2 minutes or until well blended. Let stand 2 minutes. Spread over brownie pie. Top with thawed COOL WHIP® Whipped Topping and grated chocolate, if desired. Refrigerate until ready to serve.

Makes 8 servings

Great Substitute: For an added crunch, stir in 1/2 cup chopped nuts after the flour and proceed as directed above.

Black & White Brownie Bottom Pudding Pie

Lemon Coconut Sour Cream Pie

Prep and Cook Time: 15 minutes

1 can (about 16 ounces) lemon pie filling
1 package (3.4 ounces) instant coconut cream pudding mix
1 cup sour cream
¾ cup milk
1 (6-ounce) ready-to-use graham cracker crust
¼ cup flaked coconut
Aerosol nondairy whipped topping

1. Preheat oven to 325°F. Place pie filling, pudding mix, sour cream and milk in large bowl. Beat with electric mixer at medium speed 3 to 4 minutes or until smooth. Pour into crust. Refrigerate 15 minutes.

2. While pie is chilling, spread coconut on baking sheet. Bake 8 to 10 minutes or until golden brown; cool.

3. Cover edge of pie with whipped topping. Sprinkle with coconut.

Makes 8 servings

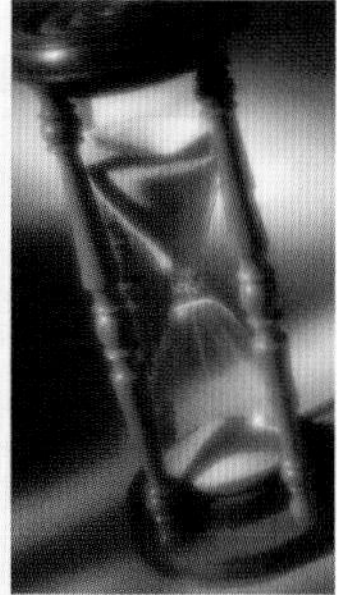

Quick Tip

When preparing this refreshing lemon pie, you can make a lighter version by using reduced-fat sour cream and low-fat or fat-free milk. Do not use fat-free sour cream, because it could change the filling consistency.

Lemon Coconut Sour Cream Pie

Texas Chocolate Peanut Butter Pie

Crust

- **1½ cups graham cracker crumbs**
- **½ cup sugar**
- **½ cup (1 stick) butter, melted**

Filling

- **16 ounces cream cheese, at room temperature**
- **2 cups creamy peanut butter**
- **1¾ cups sugar**
- **1 cup heavy whipping cream**

Topping

- **⅔ cup heavy whipping cream**
- **⅓ cup sugar**
- **½ cup (1 stick) butter**
- **3 ounces semisweet chocolate**
- **1 teaspoon vanilla extract**

For crust, preheat oven to 350°F. Combine graham cracker crumbs with sugar and melted butter. Stir until thoroughly blended. Press mixture into bottom and up side of 10-inch pie plate. Bake crust for 10 minutes; set aside to cool.

For filling, mix cream cheese, peanut butter and sugar in medium bowl until blended. Whip 1 cup cream until stiff, then fold into cream cheese mixture. Spoon filling into cooled crust.

For topping, combine ⅔ cup cream and sugar in saucepan and bring to a boil. Reduce heat and simmer for 7 minutes. Remove pan from heat. Add butter and chocolate; stir until melted. Stir in vanilla. Cool until slightly thickened. Pour evenly over pie. Refrigerate 4 to 5 hours before serving. Garnish with toasted peanuts.

Makes one 10-inch pie (8 to 10 servings)

Favorite recipe from *Texas Peanut Producers Board*

Texas Chocolate Peanut Butter Pie

Chocolate Hazelnut Torte

1 cup hazelnuts, toasted and skins removed*
3/4 cup sugar, divided
1/4 cup I CAN'T BELIEVE IT'S NOT BUTTER!® Spread
12 squares (1 ounce each) semi-sweet chocolate, divided
6 large eggs, at room temperature
1/4 cup brewed espresso coffee or coffee liqueur
1/4 cup whipping or heavy cream

**Use 1 cup whole blanched almonds, toasted, instead of hazelnuts.*

Preheat oven to 325°F. Grease 9-inch cake pan and line bottom with parchment or waxed paper; set aside.

In food processor or blender, process hazelnuts and 1/4 cup sugar until nuts are finely ground; set aside.

In top of double boiler, melt I Can't Believe It's Not Butter! Spread and 10 squares chocolate over medium heat, stirring occasionally, until smooth; set aside and let cool.

In large bowl, with electric mixer, beat eggs and remaining 1/2 cup sugar until thick and pale yellow, about 4 minutes. Beat in chocolate mixture and espresso. Stir in hazelnut mixture. Pour into prepared pan.

Bake 30 minutes or until toothpick inserted in center comes out with moist crumbs. On wire rack, cool 10 minutes; remove from pan and cool completely.

In small saucepan, bring cream to a boil. In small bowl, pour hot cream over remaining 2 squares chocolate, chopped. Stir until chocolate is melted and mixture is smooth. Pour chocolate mixture over torte to glaze. Let stand at room temperature or refrigerate until chocolate mixture is set, about 30 minutes. *Makes 8 servings*

Note: Torte may be frozen up to 1 month.

Chocolate Hazelnut Torte

Velvety Coconut and Spice Cake

Granulated sugar
2½ cups all-purpose flour
1½ teaspoons baking powder
1½ teaspoons ground cinnamon
¾ teaspoon baking soda
½ teaspoon salt
¼ teaspoon ground cloves
¼ teaspoon ground nutmeg
¼ teaspoon ground allspice
¼ teaspoon ground cardamom
½ cup (1 stick) butter, softened
½ cup packed brown sugar
4 eggs
1 teaspoon vanilla
1½ cups light cream
¼ cup molasses
1½ cups shredded coconut
Creamy Orange Frosting (recipe page 302)
⅔ cup orange marmalade
Toasted coconut for garnish

1. Preheat oven to 350°F. Grease three 8-inch round cake pans; sprinkle with enough granulated sugar to lightly coat bottoms and sides of pans.

2. Combine flour, baking powder, cinnamon, baking soda, salt, cloves, nutmeg, allspice and cardamom in bowl; set aside.

3. Beat butter in large bowl until creamy. Add ½ cup granulated sugar and brown sugar; beat until light and fluffy.

4. Add eggs, one at a time, beating well after each addition. Blend in vanilla.

5. Combine light cream and molasses in small bowl. Add flour mixture to butter mixture alternately with molasses mixture, beating well after each addition. Stir in coconut; pour evenly into prepared pans.

6. Bake 20 minutes or until wooden pick inserted in centers comes out clean. Cool in pans on wire racks 10 minutes. Loosen edges; remove to racks to cool completely.

continued on page 302

Velvety Coconut and Spice Cake

Velvety Coconut and Spice Cake, continued

7. Prepare Creamy Orange Frosting.

8. To assemble, spread two layers with marmalade; stack on cake plate.

9. Top with third layer. Frost with Creamy Orange Frosting. Refrigerate. Garnish, if desired.

Makes one 3-layer cake

Creamy Orange Frosting

1 (3-ounce) package cream cheese, softened
2 cups powdered sugar
Few drops orange extract
Milk (optional)

1. Beat cream cheese in large bowl until creamy. Gradually add powdered sugar, beating until fluffy. Blend in orange extract.

2. If necessary, add milk, 1 teaspoonful at a time, for a thinner consistency.

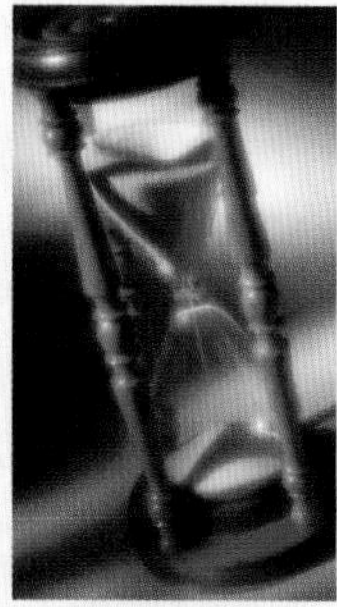

Quick Tip

To toast coconut, spread it in an even layer on a baking sheet. Place the baking sheet in a preheated 350°F oven for 8 to 10 minutes. Stir the coconut several times to ensure even toasting.

Glazed Chocolate Pound Cake

Prep Time: about 30 minutes
Bake Time: 75 to 85 minutes

Cake

1¾ cups Butter Flavor CRISCO® all-vegetable shortening or 1¾ Butter Flavor CRISCO® Stick
3 cups granulated sugar
5 eggs
1 teaspoon vanilla
3¼ cups all-purpose flour
½ cup unsweetened cocoa powder
1 teaspoon baking powder
½ teaspoon salt
1⅓ cups milk
1 cup miniature semi-sweet chocolate chips

Glaze

1 cup miniature semi-sweet chocolate chips
¼ cup Butter Flavor CRISCO® all-vegetable shortening or ¼ Butter Flavor CRISCO® Stick
1 tablespoon light corn syrup

1. For cake, heat oven to 325°F. Grease and flour 10-inch tube pan.

2. Combine 1¾ cups shortening, sugar, eggs and vanilla in large bowl. Beat at low speed of electric mixer until blended, scraping bowl constantly. Beat on high speed 6 minutes, scraping bowl occasionally. Combine flour, cocoa, baking powder and salt in medium bowl. Mix in dry ingredients alternately with milk, beating after each addition until batter is smooth. Stir in 1 cup chocolate chips. Spoon into pan.

3. Bake at 325°F for 75 to 85 minutes or until wooden pick inserted in center of cake comes out clean. Cool on cooling rack 20 minutes. Invert onto serving dish. Cool completely.

4. For glaze, combine 1 cup chocolate chips, ¼ cup shortening and corn syrup in top of double boiler over hot, not boiling water. Stir until just melted and smooth. Cool slightly. (Or place mixture in microwave-safe bowl. Microwave at 50% [Medium] for 1 minute and 15 seconds. Stir. Repeat at 15 second intervals, if necessary, until just melted and smooth. Cool slightly.) Spoon glaze over cake. Let stand until glaze is firm.

Makes 1 (10-inch) tube cake

Brandy Pecan Cake

1 cup (2 sticks) butter, softened
1¼ cups granulated sugar
¾ cup packed brown sugar
5 eggs
1 cup sour cream
½ cup brandy
2¼ cups all-purpose flour
½ cup cornmeal
2 teaspoons baking powder
1 teaspoon ground cinnamon
¼ teaspoon ground nutmeg
1 cup chopped pecans
Brandy Glaze (recipe follows)
Pecan halves for garnish

1. Preheat oven to 325°F. Generously grease and flour 10-inch tube pan.

2. Beat together butter and sugars in large bowl until light and fluffy. Add eggs, one at a time, beating well after each addition. Blend in sour cream and brandy.

3. Sift together dry ingredients. Add to butter mixture, mixing until well blended. Stir in pecans. Pour into prepared pan, spreading evenly to edges.

4. Bake 65 to 70 minutes or until wooden toothpick inserted in center of cake comes out clean. (Surface will appear slightly wet in center.)

5. Cool cake in pan on wire rack 10 minutes. Loosen edges and remove to rack to cool completely.

6. Prepare Brandy Glaze. Drizzle cake with Brandy Glaze. Garnish, if desired. Store tightly covered.

Makes one 10-inch tube cake

Brandy Glaze

2 tablespoons butter
1 cup powdered sugar
1 teaspoon brandy
4 to 5 teaspoons milk

Heat butter in medium saucepan over medium heat until melted and golden brown; cool slightly. Add powdered sugar, brandy and milk; beat until smooth.

Brandy Pecan Cake

Flourless Chocolate Cake with Raspberry Sauce

Cake

7 ounces semisweet baking chocolate, broken into pieces
12 tablespoons unsalted butter
5 eggs, separated
1 teaspoon vanilla
⅓ cup sugar
2 tablespoons unsweetened cocoa powder
⅛ teaspoon salt

Raspberry Sauce

1 package (12 ounces) frozen unsweetened raspberries, thawed
⅓ to ½ cup sugar
Additional cocoa powder for garnish

1. For cake, preheat oven to 350°F. Grease 9-inch springform pan. Heat chocolate and butter in medium saucepan over low heat until melted, stirring frequently. Remove from heat; whisk in egg yolks and vanilla. Blend in sugar, 2 tablespoons cocoa and salt.

2. Beat egg whites to soft peaks in large bowl. Stir about one fourth of the egg whites into chocolate mixture. Fold chocolate mixture into remaining egg whites.

3. Spread batter evenly in prepared pan. Bake about 30 minutes or until toothpick inserted in center comes out clean and edge of cake begins to pull away from side of pan. Cool cake in pan on wire rack 2 to 3 minutes; carefully loosen edge of cake with sharp knife and remove side of pan. Cool cake completely. Cover and refrigerate overnight or up to 3 days, or wrap well and freeze up to 3 months.

4. For sauce, blend raspberries in blender or food processor until smooth. Strain sauce and discard seeds; stir in sugar to taste. Cut cake into wedges. (If frozen, allow at least 24 hours to defrost before cutting.) Sift additional cocoa over cake; serve with sauce.

Makes 8 to 10 servings

Flourless Chocolate Cake with Raspberry Sauce

Pumpkin Spice Cake

¾ cup (1½ sticks) butter
1½ cups granulated sugar
3 eggs
1½ cups solid-pack pumpkin
1 cup buttermilk
2¾ cups all-purpose flour
1 tablespoon baking powder
1½ teaspoons baking soda
1½ teaspoons ground cinnamon
½ teaspoon salt
¼ teaspoon ground allspice
¼ teaspoon ground nutmeg
⅛ teaspoon ground ginger
Vanilla Maple Frosting (recipe follows)

1. Preheat oven to 350°F. Grease and flour two 9-inch round cake pans.

2. Beat together butter and granulated sugar in large bowl until light and fluffy. Add eggs, one at a time, beating well after each addition.

3. Combine pumpkin and buttermilk in medium bowl.

4. Sift together dry ingredients; add to butter mixture alternately with pumpkin mixture, beating well after each addition. Pour evenly into prepared pans.

5. Bake 40 to 45 minutes or until wooden toothpick inserted in centers comes out clean. Cool layers in pans on wire racks 10 minutes. Loosen edges and remove to racks to cool completely.

6. Fill and frost with Vanilla Maple Frosting. *Makes one 2-layer cake*

Vanilla Maple Frosting

1 cup (2 sticks) butter, softened
1 teaspoon vanilla
½ teaspoon maple flavoring
4 cups powdered sugar

1. Beat butter in large bowl until light and fluffy. Add vanilla and maple flavoring; mix until well blended.

2. Gradually add powdered sugar, beating until light and fluffy.

Pumpkin Spice Cake

Triple Chocolate Cake

- ¾ cup butter (1½ sticks), softened
- 1½ cups sugar
- 1 egg
- 1 teaspoon vanilla
- 2 cups all-purpose flour
- ⅔ cup unsweetened cocoa powder
- 2 teaspoons baking soda
- ¼ teaspoon salt
- 1 cup buttermilk
- ¾ cup sour cream
- Chocolate Ganache Filling (recipe follows)
- Easy Chocolate Frosting (recipe follows)

Preheat oven to 350°F. Grease and flour two 9-inch round cake pans. Beat butter and sugar in large bowl with electric mixer at medium speed until light and fluffy. Beat in egg and vanilla until blended. Combine flour, cocoa, baking soda and salt in medium bowl. Add flour mixture to butter mixture alternately with buttermilk and sour cream, beginning and ending with flour mixture. Beat well after each addition. Divide batter evenly between prepared pans.

Bake 30 to 35 minutes or until wooden toothpick inserted in centers comes out clean. Cool in pans 10 minutes. Remove from pans to wire racks; cool completely. Cut each cake layer in half horizontally.

Meanwhile, prepare Chocolate Ganache Filling. Place one cake layer on serving plate. Spread with ⅓ of filling. Repeat layers two more times. Top with remaining cake layer. Prepare Easy Chocolate Frosting; spread over cake. Garnish as desired.

Makes 1 (9-inch) layer cake

Chocolate Ganache Filling: Heat ¾ cup heavy cream, 1 tablespoon butter and 1 tablespoon granulated sugar to a boil; stir until sugar is dissolved. Place 1½ cups semisweet chocolate chips in medium bowl; pour cream mixture over chocolate and let stand 5 minutes. Stir until smooth; let stand 15 minutes or until filling reaches desired consistency. (Filling will thicken as it cools.) Makes about 1½ cups.

Easy Chocolate Frosting: Beat ½ cup softened butter in large bowl with electric mixer at medium speed until creamy. Add 4 cups powdered sugar and ¾ cup cocoa alternately with ½ cup milk; beat until smooth. Stir in 1½ teaspoons vanilla. Makes about 3 cups.

Pecan Spice Cake with Browned Butter Frosting

1 package (18 to 19 ounces) moist yellow cake mix
¾ cup sour cream
¾ cup water
3 eggs
1 tablespoon grated lemon peel
1½ teaspoons ground cinnamon
½ teaspoon ground nutmeg
¼ teaspoon ground allspice
1 cup chopped pecans
Browned Butter Frosting (recipe follows)
Additional chopped pecans (optional)

Preheat oven to 350°F. Grease two 9-inch square baking pans. Combine cake mix, sour cream, water, eggs, lemon peel and spices in large bowl with electric mixer at low speed until ingredients are moistened. Beat at high speed 2 minutes, scraping side of bowl frequently. Stir in 1 cup pecans. Divide evenly between prepared pans.

Bake 25 to 30 minutes or until wooden toothpick inserted in centers comes out clean. Cool in pans 10 minutes. Remove from pans to wire racks; cool completely. Place one layer on serving plate. Spread with ⅓ of frosting. Top with second layer. Frost sides and top of cake with remaining frosting. Garnish with additional pecans, if desired. Store tightly covered at room temperature. *Makes 12 to 16 servings*

Browned Butter Frosting

¾ cup butter
5½ cups sifted powdered sugar
8 to 9 tablespoons light cream or half-and-half
1½ teaspoons vanilla extract
Dash salt

Heat butter in heavy 1-quart saucepan over medium heat until butter is melted and light amber in color, stirring frequently. Cool butter slightly. Combine browned butter, powdered sugar, 8 tablespoons cream, vanilla and salt in large bowl. Beat on medium speed until smooth and of spreading consistency. Stir in additional 1 tablespoon cream if frosting is too stiff.

Cappuccino Cream

Prep Time: 20 minutes plus refrigerating

1 cup freshly brewed strong MAXWELL HOUSE® Coffee, at room temperature
½ cup milk
1 package (8 ounces) PHILADELPHIA® Cream Cheese, softened
1 package (4-serving size) JELL-O® Brand Vanilla Flavor Instant Pudding & Pie Filling
¼ teaspoon ground cinnamon
1 tub (8 ounces) COOL WHIP® Whipped Topping, thawed, divided
Cookies, such as biscotti or chocolate-laced pirouettes

BEAT coffee and milk gradually into cream cheese in large bowl with electric mixer on medium speed until smooth.

ADD pudding mix and cinnamon. Beat on low speed 2 minutes. Let stand 5 minutes or until thickened. Gently stir in 2 cups of COOL WHIP®. Spoon mixture into 6 dessert glasses or 1-quart serving bowl.

REFRIGERATE until ready to serve. Just before serving, top with remaining COOL WHIP®. Sprinkle with additional ground cinnamon. Serve with cookies.

Makes 6 servings

Cappuccino Cream

Spiced Cranberry-Apple Sour Cream Cobbler

4 cups cranberries, washed
6 Granny Smith apples, peeled and sliced thin
2 cups tightly packed light brown sugar
1 teaspoon ground cinnamon
1 teaspoon vanilla
¼ teaspoon ground cloves
2 cups plus 1 tablespoon all-purpose flour, divided
4 tablespoons butter, cut into bits
2 teaspoons double acting baking powder
1 teaspoon salt
½ cup CRISCO® all-vegetable shortening or ½ CRISCO® Stick
1½ cups sour cream
2 teaspoons granulated sugar

1. Heat oven to 400°F. Combine cranberries, apples, brown sugar, cinnamon, vanilla, ground cloves and 1 tablespoon flour in 3-quart baking dish; mix evenly. Dot top with butter bits.

2. Stir together remaining 2 cups flour, baking powder and salt in medium bowl. Cut shortening in using pastry blender or 2 knives until medium-size crumbs form. Add sour cream; blend well. (Dough will be sticky.) Drop dough by spoonfuls on top of fruit mixture. Sprinkle with granulated sugar. Bake at 400°F for 20 to 30 minutes, on middle rack, until top is golden. Serve with cinnamon or vanilla ice cream, if desired.

Makes 6 to 8 servings

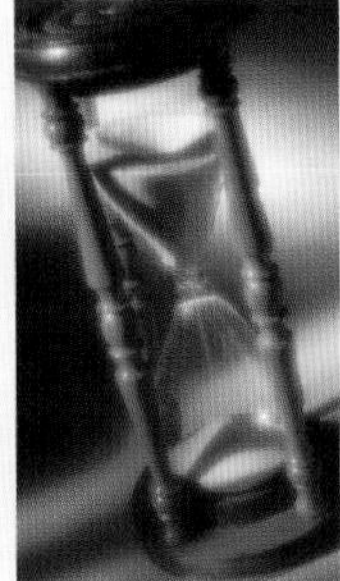

Quick Tip

Cover any leftover cobbler with foil and store it in the refrigerator for up to two days. To reheat the cobbler, place the covered baking dish in a preheated 375°F oven; bake until the cobbler is warm.

Spiced Cranberry-Apple Sour Cream Cobbler

Chocolate Passion Layered Dessert

Prep Time: 15 minutes

4 cups cold milk
2 packages (4-serving size each) JELL-O® Chocolate Flavor Instant Pudding & Pie Filling
1 package (12 ounces) pound cake, cut into cubes
¼ cup chocolate syrup or coffee liqueur, divided
1 package (12 ounces) BAKER'S® Semi-Sweet Chocolate Chunks
1 tub (8 ounces) COOL WHIP® Extra Creamy Whipped Topping, thawed

POUR milk into large bowl. Add pudding mixes. Beat with wire whisk 1 minute or until well blended.

PLACE ½ of the cake cubes in large glass serving bowl. Drizzle with ½ of the chocolate syrup. Spread ½ of the pudding over cake in bowl. Sprinkle ½ of the chunks over pudding. Spread with ½ of the whipped topping. Repeat layers. Refrigerate until ready to serve. *Makes 12 servings*

Strawberry Shortcut

Prep Time: 10 minutes

1 package (10 to 12 ounces) frozen pound cake, cut into 14 slices
3 cups strawberries, sliced, sweetened
1 tub (8 ounces) COOL WHIP® Whipped Topping, thawed

PLACE 7 of the cake slices on individual dessert plates.

SPOON about 3 tablespoons of the strawberries over each cake slice. Top each with ¼ cup whipped topping. Repeat layers, ending with a dollop of whipped topping. Garnish as desired. Serve immediately. *Makes 7 servings*

Chocolate Passion Layered Dessert

Banana Boat Sundae

HERSHEY'S Special Dark® Syrup
3 scoops vanilla ice cream
1 banana, peeled and sliced in half lengthwise
REESE'S® Shell Topping®
HERSHEY'S Classic Caramel™ Sundae Syrup
HERSHEY'S Chocolate Shoppe™ Milk Chocolate Sprinkles
HERSHEY'S Double Chocolate Sundae Syrup
REDDI-WIP® Whipped Topping

• Pour layer of HERSHEY'S Special Dark Syrup into banana split sundae dish.

• Place 3 scoops of ice cream next to each other on top of syrup. Place banana halves on each side of ice cream scoops.

• Top first ice cream scoop with REESE'S Shell Topping. Top second scoop with HERSHEY'S Classic Caramel Sundae Syrup and HERSHEY'S Chocolate Shoppe Milk Chocolate Sprinkles. Top third scoop with HERSHEY'S Double Chocolate Sundae Syrup. Top with REDDI-WIP Whipped Topping.

Makes 1 sundae

Luscious Chocolate Covered Strawberries

3 squares (1 ounce each) semi-sweet chocolate
2 tablespoons I CAN'T BELIEVE IT'S NOT BUTTER!® Spread
1 tablespoon coffee liqueur (optional)
6 to 8 large strawberries with stems

In small microwave-safe bowl, microwave chocolate and I Can't Believe It's Not Butter! Spread at HIGH (Full Power) 1 minute or until chocolate is melted; stir until smooth. Stir in liqueur. Dip strawberries in chocolate mixture, then refrigerate on waxed paper-lined baking sheet until chocolate is set, at least 1 hour.

Makes 6 to 8 strawberries

Banana Boat Sundae

Peach Cobbler

Prep Time: 20 minutes
Bake Time: 22 minutes

3 cans (16 ounces each) peach slices in juice
1 tablespoon cornstarch
2 teaspoons ground cinnamon
1 cup all-purpose flour
¼ cup packed light brown sugar
1½ teaspoons baking powder
¼ teaspoon salt
⅓ cup margarine or butter
1 large egg white
¼ cup milk

1. Preheat oven to 400°F. Drain peaches, reserving ¾ cup juice. In large bowl, combine cornstarch and cinnamon; mix well. Whisk in reserved juice, mixing until smooth. Add peaches to bowl; toss well. Transfer mixture to a shallow 1½-quart casserole or 11×7-inch baking dish.

2. In a medium bowl, combine flour, brown sugar, baking powder and salt. Cut in margarine until size of small peas. Beat together egg white and milk; mix into flour mixture until dry ingredients are just moistened. Drop batter by heaping tablespoonfuls over peaches.

3. Bake 28 to 30 minutes or until topping is golden brown and filling is bubbly. Let stand at least 15 minutes before serving. Serve warm or at room temperature.

Makes 8 servings

Peach Cobbler

Triple Chocolate Brownie Sundae

1 brownie
1 scoop chocolate ice cream
HERSHEY'S Chocolate Shell Topping
REDDI-WIP® Whipped Topping

• Place brownie on bottom of sundae dish.

• Place ice cream on top of brownie.

• Shake HERSHEY'S Chocolate Shell Topping according to instructions. Squeeze generous amount over ice cream. Allow to harden for 30 seconds.

• Top with REDDI-WIP Whipped Topping.

Makes 1 sundae

Sweetheart Chocolate Mousse

1 envelope unflavored gelatin
2 tablespoons cold water
¼ cup boiling water
1 cup sugar
½ cup HERSHEY'S Cocoa
2 cups (1 pint) cold whipping cream
2 teaspoons vanilla extract
Fresh raspberries or sliced strawberries

1. Sprinkle gelatin over cold water in small bowl; let stand 2 minutes to soften. Add boiling water; stir until gelatin is completely dissolved and mixture is clear. Cool slightly.

2. Mix sugar and cocoa in large bowl; add whipping cream and vanilla. Beat on medium speed, scraping bottom of bowl occasionally, until mixture is stiff. Pour in gelatin mixture; beat until well blended.

3. Spoon into dessert dishes. Refrigerate at least 30 minutes before serving. Garnish with fruit.

Makes about 8 servings

Triple Chocolate Brownie Sundae

Fudgy Milk Chocolate Fondue

Prep Time: 12 to 15 minutes

1 (16-ounce) can chocolate-flavored syrup
1 (14-ounce) can EAGLE® BRAND Sweetened Condensed Milk (NOT evaporated milk)
Dash salt
1½ teaspoons vanilla extract
Assorted dippers: cookies, cake, pound cake cubes, angel food cake cubes, banana chunks, apple slices, strawberries, pear slices, kiwifruit slices and/or marshmallows

1. In heavy saucepan over medium heat, combine syrup, Eagle Brand and salt. Cook and stir 12 to 15 minutes or until slightly thickened.

2. Remove from heat; stir in vanilla. Serve warm with assorted dippers. Store covered in refrigerator.

Makes about 3 cups

Microwave Directions: In 1-quart glass measure, combine syrup, Eagle Brand and salt. Microwave at HIGH (100% power) 3½ to 4 minutes, stirring after 2 minutes. Stir in vanilla.

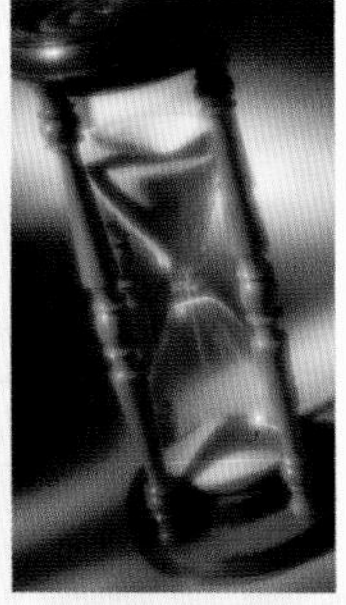

Quick Tip

Fudgy Milk Chocolate Fondue can also be served warm or cold over ice cream. Any leftover fondue can be stored, tightly covered, in the refrigerator for up to one week.

Fudgy Milk Chocolate Fondue

Chocolate Croissant Pudding

1½ cups milk
3 eggs
½ cup sugar
¼ cup unsweetened cocoa powder
½ teaspoon vanilla
¼ teaspoon salt
2 plain croissants, cut into 1-inch pieces
½ cup semisweet chocolate chips
¾ cup whipped cream (optional)

Slow Cooker Directions

1. Beat milk, eggs, sugar, cocoa, vanilla and salt in medium bowl.

2. Grease 1-quart casserole. Layer half the croissants, chocolate chips and half the egg mixture in casserole. Repeat layers with remaining croissants and egg mixture.

3. Add rack to 5-quart slow cooker and pour in 1 cup water. Place casserole on rack. Cover and cook on LOW 3 to 4 hours. Remove casserole from slow cooker. Top each serving with 2 tablespoons whipped cream, if desired. *Makes 6 servings*

Chocolate Croissant Pudding

Oatmeal Toffee Cookies

- **1 cup (2 sticks) butter or margarine, softened**
- **2 eggs**
- **2 cups packed light brown sugar**
- **2 teaspoons vanilla extract**
- **1¾ cups all-purpose flour**
- **1 teaspoon baking soda**
- **1 teaspoon ground cinnamon**
- **½ teaspoon salt**
- **3 cups quick-cooking oats**
- **1¾ cups (10-ounce package) HEATH® Almond Toffee Bits or SKOR® English Toffee Bits**
- **1 cup MOUNDS® Coconut Flakes (optional)**

1. Heat oven to 375°F. Lightly grease cookie sheet. Beat butter, eggs, brown sugar and vanilla until well blended. Add flour, baking soda, cinnamon and salt; beat until blended.

2. Stir in oats, toffee and coconut, if desired, with spoon. Drop dough by rounded teaspoons about 2 inches apart onto prepared sheet.

3. Bake 8 to 10 minutes or until edges are lightly browned. Cool 1 minute; remove to wire rack.

Makes about 4 dozen cookies

Oatmeal Toffee Cookies

Spicy Ginger Molasses Cookies

2 cups all-purpose flour
1½ teaspoons ground ginger
1 teaspoon baking soda
½ teaspoon ground cloves
¼ teaspoon salt
¾ cup (1½ sticks) butter, softened
1 cup sugar
¼ cup molasses
1 egg
Additional sugar
½ cup yogurt-covered raisins

1. Preheat oven to 375°F.

2. Combine flour, ginger, baking soda, cloves and salt in small bowl; set aside.

3. Beat butter and 1 cup sugar in large bowl of electric mixer at medium speed until light and fluffy. Add molasses and egg; beat until well blended. Gradually beat in flour mixture on low speed just until blended.

4. Drop dough by level ¼ cupfuls onto parchment-lined cookie sheets, spacing 3 inches apart. Flatten each ball of dough until 2 inches in diameter with bottom of glass that has been dipped in additional sugar. Press 7 to 8 yogurt-covered raisins into dough of each cookie.

5. Bake 11 to 12 minutes or until cookies are set. Cool cookies 2 minutes on cookie sheets; slide parchment paper and cookies onto countertop. Cool completely.

Makes about 1 dozen (4-inch) cookies

Spicy Ginger Molasses Cookies

Chocolate-Coconut-Toffee Delights

- ½ cup all-purpose flour
- ¼ teaspoon baking powder
- ¼ teaspoon salt
- 1 package (12 ounces) semisweet chocolate chips, divided
- ¼ cup butter, cut into small pieces
- ¾ cup packed light brown sugar
- 2 eggs, beaten
- 1 teaspoon vanilla
- 1½ cups flaked coconut
- 1 cup toffee baking pieces

1. Preheat oven to 350°F. Line cookie sheets with parchment paper.

2. Combine flour, baking powder and salt in small bowl; set aside. Place 1 cup chocolate chips in large microwavable bowl. Microwave at HIGH 1 minute; stir. Microwave 30 to 60 seconds more or until chips are melted; stir well.

3. Add butter to bowl; stir until melted. Beat in brown sugar, eggs and vanilla until well blended. Beat in flour mixture until blended. Stir in coconut, toffee pieces and remaining 1 cup chocolate chips.

4. Drop dough by heaping ⅓ cupfuls onto prepared cookie sheets, spacing 3 inches apart. Flatten with rubber spatula into 3½-inch circles. Bake 15 to 17 minutes or until edges are just firm to the touch. Cool cookies on cookie sheets 2 minutes; slide parchment paper and cookies onto countertop. Cool completely.

Makes 1 dozen (5-inch) cookies

Chocolate-Coconut-Toffee Delights

Easy Lemon Pudding Cookies

Prep Time: 10 minutes
Bake Time: 10 minutes

- **1 cup BISQUICK® Original Baking Mix**
- **1 package (4-serving size) JELL-O® Lemon Flavor Instant Pudding & Pie Filling**
- **½ teaspoon ground ginger (optional)**
- **1 egg, lightly beaten**
- **¼ cup vegetable oil**
- **Sugar**
- **3 squares BAKER'S® Premium White Baking Chocolate, melted**

HEAT oven to 350°F.

STIR baking mix, pudding mix and ginger in medium bowl. Mix in egg and oil until well blended. (Mixture will be stiff.) With hands, roll cookie dough into 1-inch diameter balls. Place balls 2 inches apart on lightly greased cookie sheets. Dip flat-bottom glass into sugar. Press glass onto each dough ball and flatten into ¼-inch-thick cookie.

BAKE 10 minutes or until edges are golden brown. Immediately remove from cookie sheets. Cool on wire racks. Drizzle cookies with melted white chocolate.

Makes about 20 cookies

How To Melt Chocolate: Microwave 3 squares BAKER'S® Premium White Baking Chocolate in heavy zipper-style plastic sandwich bag on HIGH 1 to 1½ minutes or until chocolate is almost melted. Gently knead bag until chocolate is completely melted. Fold down top of bag; snip tiny piece off 1 corner from bottom. Holding top of bag tightly, drizzle chocolate through opening across tops of cookies.

Easy Lemon Pudding Cookies

Butterscotch Cookies with Burnt Butter Icing

½ cup butter, softened
1½ cups packed brown sugar
2 eggs
1 teaspoon vanilla
2½ cups flour
1 teaspoon baking soda
½ teaspoon salt
1 cup dairy sour cream
1 cup finely chopped walnuts
Burnt Butter Icing (recipe follows)

Beat butter and sugar until light and fluffy. Blend in eggs and vanilla; mix well. Add combined dry ingredients alternately with sour cream, mixing well after each addition. Stir in nuts. Chill 4 hours or overnight. Drop rounded teaspoonfuls of dough, 3 inches apart, onto well buttered cookie sheets. Bake at 400°F for 8 to 10 minutes or until lightly browned. Cool on wire racks. Frost with Burnt Butter Icing.

Makes 5 dozen cookies

Burnt Butter Icing: Melt 6 tablespoons butter in small saucepan over medium heat; continue heating until golden brown. Cool. Blend in 2 cups sifted powdered sugar and 1 teaspoon vanilla. Add 2 to 3 tablespoons hot water, a little at a time, until spreading consistency is reached.

Favorite recipe from *Wisconsin Milk Marketing Board*

Hershey's® Classic Chocolate Chip Cookies

2¼ cups all-purpose flour
1 teaspoon baking soda
½ teaspoon salt
1 cup (2 sticks) butter, softened
¾ cup granulated sugar
¾ cup packed light brown sugar
1 teaspoon vanilla extract
2 eggs
2 cups (12-ounce package) HERSHEY'®S Semi-Sweet Chocolate Chips
1 cup chopped nuts (optional)

1. Heat oven to 375°F.

2. Stir together flour, baking soda and salt. Beat butter, granulated sugar, brown sugar and vanilla in large bowl with mixer until creamy. Add eggs; beat well. Gradually add flour mixture, beating well. Stir in chocolate chips and nuts, if desired. Drop by rounded teaspoons onto greased cookie sheets.

3. Bake 8 to 10 minutes or until lightly browned. Cool slightly; remove from cookie sheet to wire rack. Cool completely. *Makes 5 dozen cookies*

"Perfectly Chocolate" Chocolate Chip Cookies: Add ⅓ cup HERSHEY'®S Cocoa to flour mixture.

Pan Recipe: Spread batter into greased 15½×10½×1-inch jelly roll pan. Bake at 375°F 20 minutes or until lightly browned. Cool completely. Cut into bars. Makes about 48 bars.

Ice Cream Sandwiches: Press one small scoop of vanilla ice cream between two cookies.

High Altitude Directions: Increase flour to 2⅔ cups. Decrease baking soda to ¾ teaspoon. Decrease granulated sugar to ⅔ cup. Decrease packed light brown sugar to ⅔ cup. Add ½ teaspoon water with flour. Bake at 375°F 5 to 7 minutes or until top is light golden with golden brown edges.

Double Chocolate Cranberry Chunkies

1¾ cups all-purpose flour
⅓ cup unsweetened cocoa powder
½ teaspoon baking powder
½ teaspoon salt
1 cup (2 sticks) butter, softened
1 cup granulated sugar
½ cup packed brown sugar
1 egg
1 teaspoon vanilla
2 cups semisweet chocolate chunks or large chocolate chips
¾ cup dried cranberries or dried tart cherries
Additional granulated sugar

1. Preheat oven to 350°F.

2. Combine flour, cocoa, baking powder and salt in small bowl; set aside. Beat butter, 1 cup granulated sugar and brown sugar in large bowl of electric mixer at medium speed until light and fluffy. Beat in egg and vanilla until well blended. Gradually beat in flour mixture on low speed until blended. Stir in chocolate chunks and cranberries.

3. Drop dough by level ¼ cupfuls onto ungreased cookie sheets, spacing 3 inches apart. Flatten dough until 2 inches in diameter with bottom of glass that has been dipped in additional granulated sugar.

4. Bake 11 to 12 minutes or until cookies are set. Cool cookies 2 minutes on cookie sheets; transfer to wire racks. Cool completely. *Makes about 1 dozen (4-inch) cookies*

Double Chocolate Cranberry Chunkies

Peanut Butter Kisses

1¼ cups firmly packed light brown sugar
¾ cup creamy peanut butter
½ CRISCO® Stick or ½ cup CRISCO® all-vegetable shortening
3 tablespoons milk
1 tablespoon vanilla
1 egg
1¾ cups all-purpose flour
¾ teaspoon baking soda
¾ teaspoon salt
48 chocolate kisses, unwrapped

1. Heat oven to 375°F. Place sheets of foil on countertop for cooling cookies.

2. Combine brown sugar, peanut butter, ½ cup shortening, milk and vanilla in large bowl. Beat at medium speed of electric mixer until well blended. Add egg. Beat just until blended.

3. Combine flour, baking soda and salt. Add to shortening mixture; beat at low speed until just blended.

4. Form dough into 1-inch balls. Roll in granulated sugar. Place 2 inches apart on ungreased baking sheets.

5. Bake one baking sheet at a time at 375°F for 6 minutes. Press chocolate kiss into center of each cookie. Return to oven. Bake 3 minutes. *Do not overbake.* Cool 2 minutes on baking sheets. Remove cookies to foil to cool completely.

Makes about 3 dozen cookies

Peanut Butter Kisses

Dark Chocolate Dreams

16 ounces bittersweet chocolate candy bars or bittersweet chocolate chips
¼ cup (½ stick) butter
½ cup all-purpose flour
¾ teaspoon ground cinnamon
½ teaspoon baking powder
¼ teaspoon salt
1½ cups sugar
3 eggs
1 teaspoon vanilla
1 package (12 ounces) white chocolate chips
1 cup chopped pecans, lightly toasted

1. Preheat oven to 350°F. Grease cookie sheets.

2. Coarsely chop chocolate bars; place in microwavable bowl. Add butter. Microwave at HIGH 2 minutes; stir. Microwave 1 to 2 minutes, stirring after 1 minute, or until chocolate is melted. Cool to lukewarm.

3. Combine flour, cinnamon, baking powder and salt in small bowl; set aside.

4. Combine sugar, eggs and vanilla in large bowl of electric mixer. Beat at medium-high speed until very thick and mixture turns a pale color, about 6 minutes.

5. Reduce speed to low; slowly beat in chocolate mixture until well blended. Gradually beat in flour mixture until blended. Fold in white chocolate chips and pecans.

6. Drop batter by level ⅓ cupfuls onto prepared cookie sheets, spacing 3 inches apart. Place piece of plastic wrap over dough; flatten dough with fingertips to form 4-inch circles. Remove plastic wrap.

7. Bake 12 minutes or until just firm to the touch and surface begins to crack. *Do not overbake.* Cool cookies 2 minutes on cookie sheets; transfer to wire racks. Cool completely.

Makes 10 to 12 (5-inch) cookies

Note: Cookies may be baked on ungreased cookie sheets lined with parchment paper. Cool cookies 2 minutes on cookie sheets; slide parchment paper and cookies onto countertop. Cool completely.

Dark Chocolate Dreams

Double Chocolate Cherry Cookies

Prep Time: 25 minutes
Bake Time: 8 to 10 minutes

1¼ cups (2½ sticks) butter or margarine, softened
1¾ cups sugar
2 eggs
1 tablespoon vanilla extract
3½ cups all-purpose flour
¾ cup unsweetened cocoa
½ teaspoon baking powder
½ teaspoon baking soda
¼ teaspoon salt
2 (6-ounce) jars maraschino cherries, well drained and halved (about 60 cherries)
1 (6-ounce) package semi-sweet chocolate chips
1 (14-ounce) can EAGLE® BRAND Sweetened Condensed Milk (NOT evaporated milk)

1. Preheat oven to 350°F. In large mixing bowl, beat butter and sugar until fluffy. Add eggs and vanilla; mix well.

2. In large mixing bowl, combine dry ingredients; stir into butter mixture (dough will be stiff). Shape into 1-inch balls. Place 1 inch apart on ungreased baking sheets.

3. Press cherry half into center of each cookie. Bake 8 to 10 minutes. Cool.

4. In heavy saucepan over medium heat, melt chips with Eagle Brand; cook until mixture thickens, about 3 minutes. Frost each cookie, covering cherry. Store loosely covered at room temperature.

Makes about 10 dozen cookies

Double Chocolate Pecan Cookies: Prepare and shape dough as directed above, omitting cherries. Flatten. Bake and frost as directed. Garnish each cookie with pecan half.

Choco-Peanut Butter-Brickle Cookies

Prep Time: 15 minutes

1 (14-ounce) can EAGLE® BRAND Sweetened Condensed Milk (NOT evaporated milk)
1 cup chunky peanut butter
2 eggs
1 teaspoon vanilla extract
1½ cups all-purpose flour
1 teaspoon baking soda
½ teaspoon baking powder
½ teaspoon salt
1 cup (6 ounces) semi-sweet chocolate morsels
1 cup almond brickle chips

1. Preheat oven to 350°F. In large mixing bowl, beat Eagle Brand, peanut butter, eggs and vanilla until well blended.

2. In medium mixing bowl, combine flour, baking soda, baking powder and salt; add to peanut butter mixture, beating until blended. Stir in chocolate chips and brickle chips. Drop by heaping tablespoonfuls onto lightly greased baking sheets.

3. Bake 12 minutes or until lightly browned. Cool slightly on baking sheets; remove to wire racks to cool.

Makes 3 dozen cookies

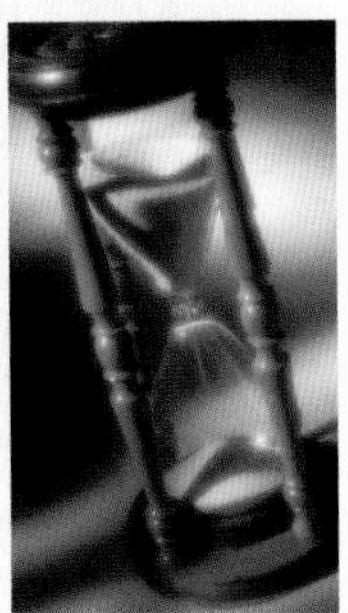

Quick Tip

When baking more than one sheet of cookies at a time, rotate the sheets from the top rack to the bottom rack and front to back about halfway through the baking time. This will result in more even baking.

Bittersweet Pecan Brownies with Caramel Sauce

Brownie

¾ cup all-purpose flour
¼ teaspoon baking soda
4 squares (1 ounce each) bittersweet or unsweetened chocolate, coarsely chopped
½ cup (1 stick) plus 2 tablespoons I CAN'T BELIEVE IT'S NOT BUTTER!® Spread
¾ cup sugar
2 eggs
½ cup chopped pecans

Caramel Sauce

¾ cup firmly packed light brown sugar
6 tablespoons I CAN'T BELIEVE IT'S NOT BUTTER!® Spread
⅓ cup whipping or heavy cream
½ teaspoon apple cider vinegar or fresh lemon juice

For brownies, preheat oven to 325°F. Line 8-inch square baking pan with aluminum foil, then grease and flour foil; set aside.

In small bowl, combine flour and baking soda; set aside.

In medium microwave-safe bowl, microwave chocolate and I Can't Believe It's Not Butter! Spread at HIGH (100% Power) 1 minute or until chocolate is melted; stir until smooth. With wooden spoon, beat in sugar, then eggs. Beat in flour mixture. Evenly spread into prepared pan; sprinkle with pecans.

Bake 31 minutes or until toothpick inserted in center comes out clean. On wire rack, cool completely. To remove brownies, lift edges of foil. Cut brownies into 4 squares, then cut each square into 2 triangles.

For caramel sauce, in medium saucepan, bring brown sugar, I Can't Believe It's Not Butter! Spread and cream just to a boil over high heat, stirring frequently. Cook 3 minutes. Stir in vinegar. To serve, pour caramel sauce around brownie and top, if desired, with vanilla or caramel ice cream. *Makes 8 servings*

Bittersweet Pecan Brownies with Caramel Sauce

Decadent Brownies

½ cup dark corn syrup
½ cup (1 stick) butter
6 squares (1 ounce each) semisweet chocolate
¾ cup sugar
3 eggs
1 cup all-purpose flour
1 cup chopped walnuts
1 teaspoon vanilla
Fudge Glaze (recipe follows)

Preheat oven to 350°F. Grease 8-inch square pan. Combine corn syrup, butter and chocolate in large heavy saucepan. Place over low heat; stir until chocolate is melted and ingredients are blended. Remove from heat; blend in sugar. Stir in eggs, flour, walnuts and vanilla. Spread batter evenly in prepared pan. Bake 20 to 25 minutes or just until center is set. *Do not overbake.* Meanwhile, prepare Fudge Glaze. Remove brownies from oven. Immediately spread glaze evenly over hot brownies. Cool in pan on wire rack. Cut into 2-inch squares. *Makes 16 brownies*

Fudge Glaze

3 squares (1 ounce each) semisweet chocolate
2 tablespoons dark corn syrup
1 tablespoon butter
1 teaspoon light cream or milk

Combine chocolate, corn syrup and butter in small heavy saucepan. Stir over low heat until chocolate is melted; mix in cream.

Decadent Brownies

Creamy Filled Brownies

- ½ cup (1 stick) butter or margarine
- ⅓ cup HERSHEY'S® Cocoa
- 2 eggs
- 1 cup sugar
- ½ cup all-purpose flour
- ¼ teaspoon baking powder
- ¼ teaspoon salt
- 1 teaspoon vanilla extract
- 1 cup finely chopped nuts
- Creamy Filling (recipe follows)
- MiniChip Glaze (recipe follows)
- ½ cup sliced almonds or chopped nuts (optional)

1. Heat oven to 350°F. Line 15½×10½×1-inch jelly-roll pan with foil; grease foil.

2. Melt butter in small saucepan; remove from heat. Stir in cocoa until smooth. Beat eggs in medium bowl; gradually add sugar, beating until fluffy. Stir together flour, baking powder and salt; add to egg mixture. Add cocoa mixture and vanilla; beat well. Stir in nuts. Spread batter into prepared pan.

3. Bake 12 to 14 minutes or until top springs back when touched lightly in center. Cool completely in pan on wire rack; remove from pan to cutting board. Remove foil; cut brownie in half crosswise. Spread one half with Creamy Filling; top with second half. Spread MiniChip Glaze over top; sprinkle with almonds, if desired. After glaze has set cut into bars.

Makes about 24 brownies

Creamy Filling: Beat 1 package (3 ounces) softened cream cheese, 2 tablespoons softened butter or margarine and 1 teaspoon vanilla extract in small bowl. Gradually add 1½ cups powdered sugar, beating until of spreading consistency.

MiniChip Glaze: Heat ¼ cup sugar and 2 tablespoons water to boiling in small saucepan. Remove from heat. Immediately add ½ cup HERSHEY'S® MINICHIPS™ Semi-Sweet Chocolate, stirring until melted.

Filling Variations: Coffee: Add 1 teaspoon powdered instant coffee. Orange: Add ½ teaspoon freshly grated orange peel and 1 or 2 drops orange food color. Almond: Add ¼ teaspoon almond extract.

Creamy Filled Brownie

Almond Brownies

½ cup (1 stick) butter
2 squares (1 ounce each) unsweetened baking chocolate
2 large eggs
1 cup firmly packed light brown sugar
¼ teaspoon almond extract
½ cup all-purpose flour
1½ cups "M&M's"® Chocolate Mini Baking Bits, divided
½ cup slivered almonds, toasted and divided
Chocolate Glaze (recipe follows)

Preheat oven to 350°F. Grease and flour 8×8×2-inch baking pan; set aside. In small saucepan melt butter and chocolate over low heat; stir to blend. Remove from heat; let cool. In medium bowl beat eggs and brown sugar until well blended; stir in chocolate mixture and almond extract. Add flour. Stir in 1 cup "M&M's"® Chocolate Mini Baking Bits and ¼ cup almonds. Spread batter evenly in prepared pan. Bake 25 to 28 minutes or until firm in center. Cool completely on wire rack. Prepare Chocolate Glaze. Spread over brownies; decorate with remaining ½ cup "M&M's"® Chocolate Mini Baking Bits and remaining ¼ cup almonds. Cut into bars. Store in tightly covered container. *Makes 16 brownies*

Chocolate Glaze: In small saucepan over low heat combine 4 teaspoons water and 1 tablespoon butter until it comes to a boil. Stir in 4 teaspoons unsweetened cocoa powder. Gradually stir in ½ cup powdered sugar until smooth. Remove from heat; stir in ¼ teaspoon vanilla extract. Let glaze cool slightly.

Almond Brownies

Blast-Off Brownies

¾ cup (1½ sticks) butter or margarine
4 (1-ounce) squares unsweetened chocolate
2 cups sugar
1 cup flour
3 eggs
1 tablespoon TABASCO® brand Pepper Sauce
½ cup semisweet chocolate chips
½ cup walnuts, chopped

Preheat oven to 350°F. Grease 9×9-inch baking pan. Melt butter and chocolate in small saucepan over medium-low heat, stirring frequently. Combine sugar, flour, eggs, TABASCO® Sauce and melted chocolate mixture in large bowl until well blended. Stir in chocolate chips and walnuts. Spoon mixture into prepared pan. Bake 35 to 40 minutes or until toothpick inserted in center comes out clean. Cool in pan on wire rack.

Makes 16 brownies

Quick Tip

A touch of heat from the addition of TABASCO® brand Pepper Sauce deepens and intensifies the chocolate flavor in these easy-to-prepare, taste-tempting brownies.

Blast-Off Brownies

Buttery Lemon Bars

Crust

1¼ cups all-purpose flour
½ cup (1 stick) butter, softened
¼ cup powdered sugar
½ teaspoon vanilla

Filling

1 cup granulated sugar
2 eggs
⅓ cup fresh lemon juice
2 tablespoons all-purpose flour
Grated peel of 1 lemon
Powdered sugar

1. Preheat oven to 350°F.

2. Combine all crust ingredients in small bowl. Beat 2 to 3 minutes until mixture is crumbly. Press onto bottom of 8-inch square baking pan. Bake 15 to 20 minutes or until edges are lightly browned.

3. Combine all filling ingredients except powdered sugar in small bowl. Beat until well mixed.

4. Pour filling over hot crust. Continue baking 15 to 18 minutes or until filling is set. Sprinkle with powdered sugar; cool completely. Cut into bars; sprinkle again with powdered sugar.

Makes about 16 bars

Toffee Bars

1 cup quick-cooking oats
½ cup all-purpose flour
½ cup firmly packed light brown sugar
½ cup finely chopped walnuts
½ cup (1 stick) butter or margarine, melted and divided
¼ teaspoon baking soda
1 (14-ounce) can EAGLE® BRAND Sweetened Condensed Milk (NOT evaporated milk)
2 teaspoons vanilla extract
2 cups (12 ounces) semi-sweet chocolate chips
Additional chopped walnuts, if desired

1. Preheat oven to 350°F. Grease 13×9-inch baking pan. In large mixing bowl, combine oats, flour, brown sugar, walnuts, 6 tablespoons butter and baking soda. Press firmly on bottom of prepared pan. Bake 10 to 15 minutes or until lightly browned.

2. Meanwhile, in medium saucepan over medium heat, combine remaining 2 tablespoons butter and Eagle Brand. Cook and stir until mixture thickens slightly, about 15 minutes. Remove from heat; stir in vanilla. Pour evenly over baked crust.

3. Bake 10 to 15 minutes or until golden brown.

4. Remove from oven; immediately sprinkle chips on top. Let stand 1 minute; spread chips while still warm. Garnish with additional walnuts, if desired; press down firmly. Cool completely. Cut into bars. Store tightly covered at room temperature.

Makes 3 dozen bars

Caramel Oatmeal Chewies

1¾ cups quick or old-fashioned oats
1¾ cups all-purpose flour, *divided*
¾ cup packed brown sugar
½ teaspoon baking soda
¼ teaspoon salt (optional)
¾ cup (1½ sticks) butter or margarine, melted
2 cups (12-ounce package) NESTLÉ® TOLL HOUSE® Semi-Sweet Chocolate Morsels
1 cup chopped nuts
1 cup caramel ice-cream topping

PREHEAT oven to 350°F. Grease bottom of 13×9-inch baking pan.

COMBINE oats, *1½ cups* flour, brown sugar, baking soda and salt in large bowl. Stir in butter; mix well. Reserve *1 cup* oat mixture; press *remaining* oat mixture onto bottom of prepared baking pan.

BAKE for 12 to 15 minutes or until golden brown. Sprinkle with morsels and nuts. Mix caramel topping with remaining flour in small bowl; drizzle over morsels to within ¼ inch of pan edges. Sprinkle with *reserved* oat mixture.

BAKE for 18 to 22 minutes or until golden brown. Cool in pan on wire rack; refrigerate until firm.

Makes about 2½ dozen bars

Chocolate Amaretto Bars

Crust

2 cups all-purpose flour
¾ cup (1½ sticks) butter or margarine, cut into pieces, softened
⅓ cup packed brown sugar

Filling

4 large eggs
¾ cup light corn syrup
¾ cup granulated sugar
¼ cup amaretto liqueur *or* ½ teaspoon almond extract
2 tablespoons butter or margarine, melted
1 tablespoon cornstarch
2 cups (about 7 ounces) sliced almonds
2 cups (12-ounce package) NESTLÉ® TOLL HOUSE® Semi-Sweet Chocolate Morsels, *divided*

PREHEAT oven to 350°F. Grease 13×9-inch baking pan.

For Crust
BEAT flour, butter and sugar in large mixer bowl until crumbly. Press into prepared baking pan. Bake for 12 to 15 minutes or until golden brown.

For Filling
BEAT eggs, corn syrup, sugar, liqueur, butter and cornstarch in medium bowl with wire whisk. Stir in almonds and *1⅔ cups* morsels. Pour over hot crust; spread evenly. Bake for 25 to 30 minutes or until center is set. Cool in pan on wire rack.

For Chocolate Drizzle
PLACE *remaining* morsels in *heavy-duty* plastic bag. Microwave on HIGH (100% power) for 30 to 45 seconds; knead. Microwave at 10- to 20-second intervals, kneading until smooth. Cut tiny corner from bag; squeeze to drizzle over bars. Refrigerate for a few minutes to firm chocolate before cutting into bars.

Makes about 2½ dozen bars

S'more Snack Treats

Preparation Time: 15 minutes
Cook Time: 20 minutes
Chill Time: 20 minutes
Total Time: 55 minutes

44 HONEY MAID® Honey Graham squares
3 tablespoons margarine or butter
1 (10-ounce) package JET-PUFFED® Marshmallows
¾ cup miniature semisweet chocolate chips

1. Break grahams into bite-size pieces; set aside.

2. Heat margarine or butter in large saucepan over medium heat until melted. Add marshmallows, stirring constantly until melted.

3. Stir broken crackers into marshmallow mixture to coat evenly. Spread mixture into lightly greased 13×9×2-inch pan; sprinkle with chocolate chips, pressing lightly with greased hands.

4. Refrigerate at least 20 minutes before cutting into squares.

Makes 12 s'mores

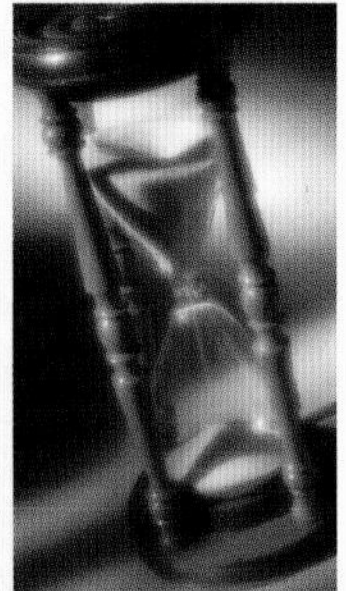

Quick Tip

These no-bake snack treats are oh-so simple to prepare—and you don't have to turn on the oven. With only four ingredients and quick cleanup, these kid-pleasing treats can be ready in no time.

S'more Snack Treats

Peanut Butter Ice Cream Triangles

- 1½ cups all-purpose flour
- ½ teaspoon baking powder
- ½ teaspoon baking soda
- ¼ teaspoon salt
- ½ cup (1 stick) butter, softened
- ½ cup granulated sugar
- ½ cup packed brown sugar
- ½ cup creamy peanut butter
- 1 egg
- 1 teaspoon vanilla
- 2½ to 3 cups vanilla, cinnamon or chocolate ice cream, softened

1. Preheat oven to 350°F. Grease cookie sheets.

2. Combine flour, baking powder, baking soda and salt in small bowl; set aside. Beat butter, granulated sugar and brown sugar in large bowl of electric mixer at medium speed until light and fluffy. Beat in peanut butter, egg and vanilla until well blended. Gradually beat in flour mixture on low speed until blended.

3. Divide dough in half. Roll each piece of dough between 2 sheets of waxed paper or plastic wrap into 10×10-inch square, about ⅛ inch thick. Remove top sheet of waxed paper; invert dough onto prepared cookie sheet. Remove second sheet of waxed paper.

4. Score dough into four 4-inch squares. Score each square diagonally into two triangles. *Do not cut completely through dough.* Repeat with remaining dough. Combine excess scraps of dough; roll out and score into additional triangles. Pierce each triangle with fork.

5. Bake 12 to 13 minutes or until set and edges are golden brown. Cool cookies 2 minutes on cookie sheets. Cut through score marks with knife; cool completely on cookie sheets.

6. Place half the cookies on flat surface. Spread ¼ to ⅓ cup softened ice cream on flat side of each cookie; top with remaining cookies. Wrap in plastic wrap and freeze 1 hour or up to 2 days.

Makes about 10 ice cream sandwiches

Peanut Butter Ice Cream Triangle

Chocolate Chip Caramel Bars

- 1 Butter Flavor CRISCO® Stick or 1 Butter Flavor CRISCO® all-vegetable shortening plus additional for greasing
- 1 cup granulated sugar
- ½ cup firmly packed light brown sugar
- 2 eggs
- 2 teaspoons vanilla
- 2 cups all-purpose flour
- 1 teaspoon baking soda
- 1 teaspoon salt
- 2 cups (12-ounce package) semi-sweet chocolate chips
- 1 bag (14 ounces) caramels, unwrapped
- 2 tablespoons cold water

1. Heat oven to 350°F. Grease 8×8×2-inch pan with shortening. Flour lightly. Place cooling rack on countertop.

2. Combine shortening, granulated sugar, brown sugar, eggs and vanilla in large bowl. Beat at medium speed of electric mixer until blended.

3. Combine flour, baking soda and salt. Add gradually to creamed mixture at low speed. Beat until well blended. Stir in chocolate chips with spoon. Divide dough in half. Spread half in bottom of prepared pan.

4. Combine caramels and water in small saucepan. Place on very low heat. Stir until caramels melt. Spread over dough in pan to within ½ inch of edge. Spoon remaining dough over caramel mixture. Spread carefully.

5. Bake at 350°F for 15 to 20 minutes or until golden brown. Loosen from sides of pan with knife. Remove pan to cooling rack to cool completely. Cut into bars about 1½×1½ inches.

Makes about 2 dozen bars

Chocolate Fudge Pecan Bars

2⅔ cups all-purpose flour
1¼ cups packed light brown sugar, divided
1 cup (2 sticks) cold butter or margarine
4 eggs
1 cup light corn syrup
4 bars (1 ounce each) HERSHEY®'S Unsweetened Baking Chocolate, unwrapped and melted
2 teaspoons vanilla extract
½ teaspoon salt
2 cups coarsely chopped pecans

1. Heat oven to 350°F. Grease 15½×10½×1-inch jelly-roll pan.

2. Stir together flour and ¼ cup brown sugar in large bowl. With pastry blender, cut in butter until mixture resembles coarse crumbs; press onto bottom of prepared pan.

3. Bake 10 to 15 minutes or until set. Remove from oven. With back of spoon, lightly press crust into corners and against sides of pan.

4. Beat eggs, corn syrup, remaining 1 cup brown sugar, melted chocolate, vanilla and salt; stir in pecans. Pour mixture evenly over warm crust. Return to oven.

5. Bake 25 to 30 minutes or until chocolate filling is set. Cool completely in pan on wire rack. Cut into bars. *Makes about 36 bars*

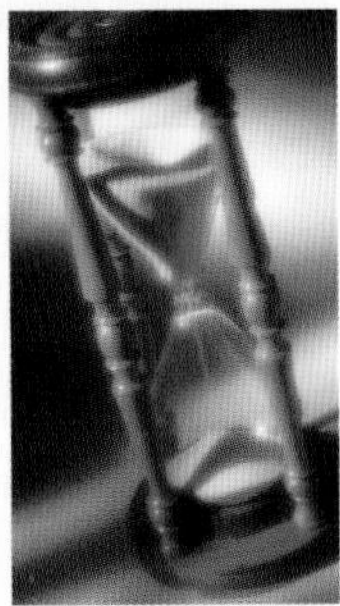

Quick Tip

Chocolate Fudge Pecan Bars will remind you of an old favorite, pecan pie. The added dimension here is the chocolate in the filling. They are special enough for guests but easy to fix for an everyday family dessert.

Chocolate Chip Candy Cookie Bars

- 1⅔ cups all-purpose flour
- 2 tablespoons plus 1½ cups sugar, divided
- ¾ teaspoon baking powder
- 1 cup (2 sticks) cold butter or margarine, divided
- 1 egg, slightly beaten
- ½ cup plus 2 tablespoons (5-ounce can) evaporated milk, divided
- 2 cups (12-ounce package) HERSHEY®S Semi-Sweet Chocolate Chips, divided
- ½ cup light corn syrup
- 1½ cups sliced almonds

1. Heat oven to 375°F.

2. Stir together flour, 2 tablespoons sugar and baking powder in medium bowl; using pastry blender, cut in ½ cup butter until mixture forms coarse crumbs. Stir in egg and 2 tablespoons evaporated milk; stir until mixture holds together in ball shape. Press onto bottom and ¼-inch up sides of 15½×10½×1-inch jelly-roll pan.

3. Bake 8 to 10 minutes or until lightly browned; remove from oven, leaving oven on. Sprinkle 1½ cups chocolate chips evenly over crust; do not disturb chips.

4. Place remaining 1½ cups sugar, remaining ½ cup butter, remaining ½ cup evaporated milk and corn syrup in 3-quart saucepan. Cook over medium heat, stirring constantly, until mixture boils; stir in almonds. Continue cooking and stirring to 240°F on candy thermometer (soft-ball stage) or until small amount of mixture, when dropped into very cold water, forms a soft ball which flattens when removed from water. (Bulb of candy thermometer should not rest on bottom of saucepan.) Remove from heat. Immediately spoon almond mixture evenly over chips and crust; do not spread.

5. Bake 10 to 15 minutes or just until almond mixture is golden brown. Remove from oven; cool 5 minutes. Sprinkle remaining ½ cup chips over top; cool completely. Cut into bars.

Makes about 48 bars

Chocolate Chip Candy Cookie Bars

Oatmeal Hermits

3 cups QUAKER® Oats (quick or old fashioned, uncooked)
1 cup all-purpose flour
1 cup (2 sticks) butter or margarine, melted
1 cup firmly packed brown sugar
1 cup raisins
½ cup chopped nuts
1 egg
¼ cup milk
1 teaspoon vanilla
1 teaspoon ground cinnamon
½ teaspoon baking soda
½ teaspoon salt (optional)
¼ teaspoon ground nutmeg

Heat oven to 375°F. In large bowl, combine all ingredients; mix well. Drop by rounded tablespoonfuls onto ungreased cookie sheets. Bake 8 to 10 minutes. Cool 1 minute on cookie sheets; remove to wire cooling rack. *Makes about 3 dozen*

For Bar Cookies: Press dough into ungreased 15×10-inch jelly-roll pan. Bake about 17 minutes or until golden brown. Cool completely; cut into bars.

Quick Tip

When baking cookies, always cool cookie sheets completely before reusing them. Placing cookie dough on hot sheets will cause the dough to begin spreading before baking.

Acknowledgments

The publisher would like to thank the companies and organizations listed below for the use of their recipes and photographs in this pubication.

A.1.® Steak Sauce
Barilla America, Inc.
BelGioioso® Cheese, Inc.
Bob Evans®
California Wild Rice Advisory Board
Chef Paul Prudhomme's Magic Seasoning Blends®
ConAgra Foods®
Cucina Classica Italiana, Inc.
Del Monte Corporation
Dole Food Company, Inc.
Eagle® Brand
Filippo Berio® Olive Oil
Fleischmann's® Original Spread
Fleischmann's® Yeast
The Golden Grain Company®
Hershey Foods Corporation
The Hidden Valley® Food Products Company
Hillshire Farm®
Holland House® is a registered trademark of Mott's, Inc.
HONEY MAID® Honey Grahams
Hormel Foods, LLC
Keebler® Company
Kellogg Company
Kraft Foods Holdings
Lawry's® Foods, Inc.
© Mars, Incorporated 2002
McIlhenny Company (TABASCO® brand Pepper Sauce)
Michigan Apple Committee
Nabisco Biscuit and Snack Division
National Honey Board
National Pork Board
National Turkey Federation
Nestlé USA
North Dakota Wheat Commission
Pear Bureau Northwest
Perdue Farms Incorporated
PLANTERS® Nuts
The Quaker® Oatmeal Kitchens
Reckitt Benckiser
RED STAR® Yeast, a product of Lasaffre Yeast Corporation
Reddi-wip® is a registered trademark of ConAgra Brands, Inc.
Sargento® Foods Inc.
Sauder's Penn Dutch Eggs
The J.M. Smucker Company
StarKist® Seafood Company
The Sugar Association, Inc.
Sunkist Growers, Inc.
Texas Peanut Producers Board
Uncle Ben's Inc.
Unilever Bestfoods North America
USA Rice Federation
Wisconsin Milk Marketing Board

Notes